	DATE DUE	

THREE PLAYS

Anton Chekhov

Three Plays

The Sea-Gull, Three Sisters & The Cherry Orchard

Translated by Constance Garnett

Introduction by Kenneth Rexroth

THE MODERN LIBRARY

NEW YORK

2001 Modern Library Edition

Introduction copyright © 1967 by Kenneth Rexroth
Biographical note copyright © 2001 by Random House, Inc.

LIBRARY OF CONGRESS CATALOGING-IN-PUBLICATION DATA
Chekhov, Anton Pavlovich, 1860–1904.
[Plays. English. Selections]
Three plays / Anton Chekhov ; translated by Constance Garnett ;
introduction by Kenneth Rexroth.
p. cm.
Contents: The Sea-gull—Three sisters—The cherry orchard.
ISBN 0-679-64235-8
1. Chekhov, Anton Pavlovich, 1860–1904—Translations into English. I. Garnett,
Constance Black, 1862–1946. II. Title.
PG3456.A19 2001
891.72'3—dc21   2001032961

Modern Library website address: www.modernlibrary.com

Printed in the United States of America

2   4   6   8   9   7   5   3   1

ANTON CHEKHOV

Anton Pavlovich Chekhov was born on January 17, 1860, in Taganrog, a small provincial port in southern Russia located on the Sea of Azov. His grandfather had been a serf who for 3,500 rubles had purchased the family's freedom. Chekhov's domineering father was a lower-middle-class bigot: a petty merchant who kept a grocery store, bullied his wife, and beat his six children. Although Anton Pavlovich's early life was monotonous and oppressive ("In my childhood there was no childhood," the writer recalled), he found his own strange way of compensating for the dismal atmosphere. Possessing a natural gift for clowning and mimicry, the boy delighted schoolmates with hilarious imitations of virtually everyone in the village. (Much as in his later stories, things for him were funny and sad at the same time, but you would not see their sadness if you did not see their fun, because both were linked up.)

Chekhov was sixteen when the family business failed and his father escaped debtors' prison by fleeing to Moscow. The young man's mother and siblings soon followed, but Anton Pavlovich remained behind to complete his education at the Taganrog Secondary School; three years later, in 1879, he joined them in Moscow and entered the medical faculty of Moscow University. During his university years Chekhov became the family's chief breadwinner: He supported them by writing stories, sketches, and parodies for humor magazines. All his early works were signed with pseudonyms, most frequently "Antosha Chekhonte." He completed medical school in 1884 and practiced medicine intermittently for several years while continuing to write. "Medicine is my lawful wife," Chekhov wrote to a friend, "and literature is my mistress. When I get fed up with one, I spend the night with the other. Though it is irregular, it is less boring this way, and besides, neither of them loses anything through my infidelity."

All the while, Chekhov's fiction continued to grow in depth and range. He published his first volume of stories, *Motley Stories,* in 1886; a year later he brought out his second collection, *In the Twilight,* for which he was awarded the Pushkin Prize for distinguished literary achievement by the Russian Academy. Fellow countryman Vladimir Nabokov perfectly explained Chekhov's appeal: "What really attracted the Russian reader was that in Chekhov's heroes he recognized the Russian idealist ... a man who combined the deepest human decency of which man is capable with an almost ridiculous inability to put his ideals and principles into action; a man devoted to moral beauty, the welfare of his people, the welfare of the universe, but unable in his private life to do anything useful; frittering away his provincial existence in a haze of utopian dreams; knowing exactly what is good, what is worth while living for, but at the same time sinking lower and lower in the mud of a humdrum existence, unhappy in love, hopelessly inefficient in everything—a good man who cannot make good. This is the character that passes—in the guise of a doctor, a student, a village teacher, many other professional people—all through Chekhov's stories."

Despite the success of his literary career, Chekhov felt guilty about neglecting medicine. Moreover, he still owed a dissertation to obtain a full M.D. Partly to discharge this debt, partly for the sake of adventure, Chekhov in 1890 undertook an exhausting—and at times dangerous—six-thousand-mile journey (prerailroad) across Siberia to Sakhalin Island. There he made a thorough study of social, economic, and medical conditions, both of the Russian settlers (mostly convicts) and of native populations. Upon his return (by sea, via the Suez Canal) from this "descent into hell," circumstances quickly forced him back into medicine and public health service—first the terrible famine of 1891 and then the cholera epidemic that followed. In 1892 Chekhov bought a six-hundred-acre country estate near the village of Melihovo, where for the next five years he served as doctor to the local peasants and even helped build schools, while his literary output continued unabated.

The turn of the century witnessed a dramatic new phase in Chekhov's career. Between 1896 and 1903 he wrote the plays that established his reputation as one of the great dramatists of modern times: *The Sea-Gull* (1896), *Uncle Vanya* (1897), *Three Sisters* (1901), and *The Cherry Orchard* (1904). However, in 1897 a massive pulmonary hemorrhage forced him finally to acknowledge that he was stricken with tuberculosis, an illness he had long concealed. For the remainder of his life, Chekhov was virtually a semi-invalid; he lived mostly in a villa at Yalta, his "warm Siberia" where he met Tolstoy and Gorky. In 1901 Chekhov married Olga Knipper, an actress with the Moscow Art Theater who had played the role of Irina in *The Sea-Gull*.

Chekhov's last public appearance took place at the Moscow premiere of *The Cherry Orchard* on January 17, 1904, the playwright's forty-fourth birthday. Shaken with coughing, he was hardly able to stand and acknowledge a thunderous ovation. In June Chekhov was rushed to a health resort at Badenweiler in the Black Forest, where he died of consumption on July 2. His body was transported back to Moscow in a refrigerating car used for the transportation of oysters— a quirk of fate that no doubt he would have been amused to jot down in his notebook.

CONTENTS

Introduction

Kenneth Rexroth

It comes as a bit of a shock to sit yourself down and deliberately think, "In the first half of the twentieth century, the position once occupied in ancient Greece by Aeschylus, Sophocles, and Euripides was held, in the estimation of those who sought serious satisfaction in the modern theater, by Ibsen, Strindberg, and Chekhov." What had happened in two thousand years? Had it happened to the audiences, or to the playwrights, or to the self-evolving art of drama? Or was the change more profound than this, more profound even than a change in the meaning of civilization—was it a change in the very nature of man? We still say we enjoy *Antigone;* but if we go directly from a performance of that play to Chekhov's *Three Sisters,* it is difficult not to believe that the men of Classic times were different from us, a different kind of men.

In certain plays, both Ibsen and Strindberg set out deliberately to compete with the great past, with Shakespeare or Schiller or Sophocles or Aeschylus. The results are hardly competition. *Peer Gynt* or *Damascus* bears little resemblance to the past, though certain Strindberg plays do contain distorted reflections of Euripides. But Chekhov—what would the Greeks have made of *The Sea-Gull?* They would have classed it with Menander, with the New Comedy of domestic conflict and absurd situation. So did Chekhov. We seldom pay attention to half-titles in "Collected Plays," but there it says, right on the page—*"The Sea-Gull, A Comedy in Four Acts." Ivanov* is called "a drama"; *Uncle Vanya,* "scenes of country life"; *Three Sisters,* a "drama"; *The Cherry Orchard,* certainly the saddest of all, "A comedy."

So simply Chekhov states his aesthetic, and with it a philosophy of life. If we take these heartbreaking plays as tragedies in the sense in which *Oedipus the King* is a tragedy, we are self-convicted of sentimentality. No one has ever had a more delicate sentiment, a more careful sensibility, when it comes to portraying, and so judging, the lives of more-than-ordinary men and women—but no one was ever less a sentimentalist—than Chekhov. This is why he outraged a swashbuckling sentimentalist like D. H. Lawrence, who hated him and who couldn't understand why he didn't come down hard on the right side and plump for the Good Guys and The Life Force.

Chekhov always insisted that the five plays of his maturity that his audiences insisted were tragedies were simply developments, precisely in maturity, of the hilarious short farces of his youth. But if Irina's "Moscow, Moscow, we'll never see Moscow now!" is not tragic, then Chekhov is mocking us, and his characters—and, not least, his actors—too. No. Chekhov is the master of an art of such highly refined modesty that he can present his people in their simplicity on a stage and let life itself do the mocking.

He wanted a new theater, a theater that would tell it the way it really was. There has been plenty of realist and naturalist theater in Russia in his day and since, but there is only one Chekhov. The naturalist theater uses a whole armamentarium of devices to create an illusion of "real life" and then drive home its points, all derived from the storehouse of literary and dramatic morality.

There have been many more lifelike plays than Chekhov's. His is not a circumstantial naturalism of décor and talk and event—it is a moral naturalism. These lost people, off in the vast provinces of Russia, frustrated, aimless, hopeless, or full of utopian unrealizable hopes, all alike coming to trivial ends, actually make up a highly stylized theater of their own, as formal or classic as the Commedia dell' Arte or Plautus and Terence.

What is realistic, or naturalistic? What is "life as it really is"? This is the silent moral commentary that underlines every speech, like an unheard organ pedal. Is it a judgment? In the sense in which "Judge not lest ye be judged" is a judgment.

There is something intrinsically ridiculous about all the people in all the plays. Chekhov's is truly a theater of the absurd. Yet we never think of them as very funny—and we don't think of them as very sad, either. The play as a whole may sadden us, as life saddens us with all the massive pathos of mortality, but Chekhov's people we simply accept.

We do not judge Irina to be a silly girl or Trigorin to be an ass and a cad, although they certainly say foolish and silly and asinine things. And when that recurrent character who always says, "Some day life will be splendid, and people in those far-off days will look back on us and pity us in our filth and misery and thank us for having endured our agonies for them, so that they might be" speaks his recurrent part, we neither laugh nor sigh nor believe, but at the most think, "Perhaps. Not likely. It won't matter."

Chekhov would have been horrified if anyone had cold-bloodedly accused him of teaching a moral—but so he does. We accept these tragic comedies, these sorrowful farces of Chekhov's the way we would accept life itself if we were gifted with sudden wisdom. Chekhov places us in a situation, confronting the behavior of a number of human beings in what seems to them, at least, an important crisis. We are so placed, so situated and informed, that we can afford to be wise. We can regard the affairs of men as they should be regarded, in the aspect of timelessness. But this is what Sophocles does.

Once we accept both the idiom of Chekhov and the idiom of Sophocles we can compare them, and we can see very clearly the great precision and economy with which Chekhov works. His plays are pre-eminently, in modern times, playwright's plays, a joy for a fellow craftsman to see or read. How right everything is! How little time or speech is wasted! How much every line is saturated with action! Sophocles, Molière, Racine—very few other playwrights have been as accurate and as economical.

It is this genius for stating only the simplest truth as simply as can be that makes Chekhov inexhaustible—like life. We can see him for the hundredth time when we are sick of everything else in the theater, just as we can read his stories when everything else, even detectives and science fiction, bores us. We are not bored because we do not feel we are being manipulated. We are, of course, but manipulated to respond, "That's the way it is." Since the professional manipulators of the mind never have this response in view, we are quite unconscious of Chekhov's craftiness—that he is always interfering on the side of suspended judgment.

Quite unlike those of Ibsen and Strindberg, who were tireless preachers and manipulators, Chekhov's people are not alienated. They have trouble, as men have always had, communicating, but the cast of each play forms a community nonetheless. They would all like to live in a society of mutual aid if only they could define the means and ends of aid itself. One feels that Ibsen and Strindberg didn't like any of their casts very much and made them up of people who wouldn't listen to Ibsen and Strindberg. Chekhov doesn't want to be listened to. He isn't there. He is out of sight, in the last row of the balcony, listening. "I imagine people so they can tell me things about themselves." This is an unusual, but certainly an unusually effective, credo for a playwright.

It is easy to accept Orestes or Hamlet as an archetype. Hundreds of books are written analyzing the new pantheon of heroes who make up the inner dramas of our unconscious. They are very spectacular personages, these. It is hard at first to believe a playwright who comes to us and says, "The schoolteacher and the two stenographers next door to where you live in Fort Dodge—these are the real archetypes." But until we have learned this—and most of us will never learn it, however many Chekhov plays we see; not really, not deep in the bowels of compassion, but only as we learn things in books—we will never learn to approach life with the beginnings of wisdom: with that wisdom so characteristic of Sophocles.

THE SEA-GULL

First performed in St. Petersburg,

October 1896

CHARACTERS IN THE PLAY

IRINA NIKOLAYEVNA ARKADIN (MADAME TREPLEV) (*an actress*).
KONSTANTIN GAVRILOVITCH TREPLEV (*her son, a young man*).
PYOTR NIKOLAYETVITCH SORIN (*her brother*).
NINA MIHAILOVNA ZARETCHNY (*a young girl, the daughter of a wealthy landowner*).
ILYA AFANASYEVITCH SHAMRAEV (*a retired lieutenant, SORIN'S steward*).
POLINA ANDREYEVNA (*his wife*).
MASHA (*his daughter*).
BORIS ALEXEYEVITCH TRIGORIN (*a literary man*).
YEVGENY SERGEYEVITCH DORN (*a doctor*).
SEMYON SEMYONOVITCH MEDVEDENKO (*a schoolmaster*).
YAKOV (*a labourer*).
A MAN COOK.
A HOUSEMAID.

The action takes place in SORIN'S house and garden. Between the Third and Fourth Acts there is an interval of two years.

ACT I

Part of the park on SORIN'S *estate. Wide avenue leading away from the specta-
tors into the depths of the park towards the lake is blocked up by a platform
roughly put together for private theatricals, so that the lake is not visible. To right
and left of the platform, bushes. A few chairs, a little table.*

The sun has just set. YAKOV *and other labourers are at work on the platform
behind the curtain; there is the sound of coughing and hammering.* MASHA *and*
MEDVEDENKO *enter on the left, returning from a walk.*

MEDVEDENKO. Why do you always wear black?

MASHA. I am in mourning for my life. I am unhappy.

MEDVEDENKO. Why? (*Pondering*) I don't understand ... You are in good
health; though your father is not very well off, he has got enough.
My life is much harder than yours. I only get twenty-three roubles
a month, and from that they deduct something for the pension
fund, and yet I don't wear mourning. (*They sit down.*)

MASHA. It isn't money that matters. A poor man may be happy.

MEDVEDENKO. Theoretically, yes; but in practice it's like this: there are
my two sisters and my mother and my little brother and I, and my
salary is only twenty-three roubles. We must eat and drink, mustn't
we? One must have tea and sugar. One must have tobacco. It's a
tight fit.

MASHA (*looking round at the platform*). The play will soon begin.

MEDVEDENKO. Yes. Miss Zaretchny will act: it is Konstantin Gavrilitch's play. They are in love with each other and to-day their souls
will be united in the effort to realise the same artistic effect. But
your soul and mine have not a common point of contact. I love you.
I am so wretched I can't stay at home. Every day I walk four miles
here and four miles back and I meet with nothing but indifference
from you. I can quite understand it. I am without means and have a

big family to keep.... Who would care to marry a man who hasn't a
penny to bless himself with?

MASHA. Oh, nonsense! (*Takes a pinch of snuff*) Your love touches me,
but I can't reciprocate it—that's all. (*Holding out the snuff-box to him*)
Help yourself.

MEDVEDENKO. I don't feel like it (*a pause*).

MASHA. How stifling it is! There must be a storm coming.... You're always discussing theories or talking about money. You think there is
no greater misfortune than poverty, but to my mind it is a thousand
times better to go in rags and be a beggar than ... But you wouldn't
understand that, though....

(SORIN *and* TREPLEV *enter on the right.*)

SORIN (*leaning on his walking-stick*). I am never quite myself in the
country, my boy, and, naturally enough, I shall never get used to it.
Last night I went to bed at ten and woke up this morning at nine
feeling as though my brain were glued to my skull, through sleeping so long (*laughs*). And after dinner I accidentally dropped off
again, and now I am utterly shattered and feel as though I were in a
nightmare, in fact....

TREPLEV. Yes, you really ought to live in town. (*Catches sight of* MASHA
and MEDVEDENKO) When the show begins, my friends, you will be
summoned, but you mustn't be here now. You must please go away.

SORIN (*to* MASHA). Marya Ilyinishna, will you be so good as to ask your
papa to tell them to take the dog off the chain?—it howls. My sister
could not sleep again last night.

MASHA. Speak to my father yourself; I am not going to. Please don't
ask me. (*To* MEDVEDENKO) Come along!

MEDVEDENKO (*to* TREPLEV). So you will send and let us know before it
begins. (*Both go out.*)

SORIN. So I suppose the dog will be howling all night again. What a
business it is! I have never done as I liked in the country. In old days
I used to get leave for twenty-eight days and come here for a rest
and so on, but they worried me so with all sorts of trifles that before
I had been here two days I was longing to be off again (*laughs*). I've
always been glad to get away from here.... But now I am on the re-

tired list, and I have nowhere else to go, as a matter of fact. I've got to live here whether I like it or not....

YAKOV (*to* TREPLEV). We are going to have a bathe, Konstantin Gavrilitch.

TREPLEV. Very well; but don't be more than ten minutes (*looks at his watch*). It will soon begin.

YAKOV. Yes, sir (*goes out*).

TREPLEV (*looking round the stage*). Here is our theatre. The curtain, then the first wing, then the second, and beyond that—open space. No scenery of any sort. There is an open view of the lake and the horizon. We shall raise the curtain at exactly half-past eight, when the moon rises.

SORIN. Magnificent.

TREPLEV. If Nina is late it will spoil the whole effect. It is time she was here. Her father and her stepmother keep a sharp eye on her, and it is as hard for her to get out of the house as to escape from prison (*puts his uncle's cravat straight*). Your hair and your beard are very untidy. They want clipping or something....

SORIN (*combing out his beard*). It's the tragedy of my life. Even as a young man I looked as though I had been drinking for days or something of the sort. I was never a favourite with the ladies (*sitting down*). Why is your mother out of humour?

TREPLEV. Why? Because she is bored (*sitting down beside him*). She is jealous. She is set against me, and against the performance, and against my play because Nina is acting in it, and she is not. She does not know my play, but she hates it.

SORIN (*laughs*). What an idea!

TREPLEV. She is annoyed to think that even on this little stage Nina will have a triumph and not she (*looks at his watch*). My mother is a psychological freak. Unmistakably talented, intelligent, capable of sobbing over a book, she will reel off all Nekrassov by heart; as a sick nurse she is an angel; but just try praising Duse in her presence! O-ho! You must praise no one but herself, you must write about her, make a fuss over her, be in raptures over her extraordinary acting in "La Dame aux Camélias" or the "Ferment of Life"; but she has none of this narcotic in the country, she is bored and cross, and we are all her enemies—we are all in fault. Then she is superstitious—she is afraid of three candles, of the number thirteen. She is stingy. She has got seventy thousand roubles in a bank at Odessa—I know that for a fact—but ask her to lend you some money, and she will burst into tears.

SORIN. You imagine your mother does not like your play, and you are already upset and all that. Don't worry; your mother adores you.

TREPLEV (*pulling the petals off a flower*). Loves me, loves me not; loves me, loves me not; loves me, loves me not (*laughs*). You see, my mother does not love me. I should think not! She wants to live, to love, to wear light blouses; and I am twenty-five, and I am a continual reminder that she is no longer young. When I am not there she is only thirty-two, but when I am there she is forty-three, and for that she hates me. She knows, too, that I have no belief in the theatre. She loves the stage, she fancies she is working for humanity, for the holy cause of art, while to my mind the modern theatre is nothing but tradition and conventionality. When the curtain goes up, and by artificial light, in a room with three walls, these great geniuses, the devotees of holy art, represent how people eat, drink, love, move about, and wear their jackets; when from these commonplace sentences and pictures they try to draw a moral—a petty moral, easy of comprehension and convenient for domestic use; when in a thousand variations I am offered the same thing over and over again—I run away as Maupassant ran away from the Eiffel Tower which weighed upon his brain with its vulgarity.

SORIN. You can't do without the stage.

TREPLEV. We need new forms of expression. We need new forms, and if we can't have them we had better have nothing (*looks at his watch*). I love my mother—I love her very much—but she leads a senseless sort of life, always taken up with this literary gentleman, her name is always trotted out in the papers—and that wearies me. And sometimes the simple egoism of an ordinary mortal makes me feel sorry that my mother is a celebrated actress, and I fancy that if she were an ordinary woman I should be happier. Uncle, what could be more hopeless and stupid than my position? She used to have visitors, all celebrities—artists and authors—and among them all I was the only one who was nothing, and they only put up with me because I was her son. Who am I? What am I? I left the

University in my third year—owing to circumstances "for which we accept no responsibility," as the editors say; I have no talents, I haven't a penny of my own, and on my passport I am described as an artisan of Kiev. You know my father was an artisan of Kiev, though he too was a well-known actor. So, when in her drawing-room all these artists and authors graciously noticed me, I always fancied from their faces that they were taking the measure of my insignificance—I guessed their thoughts and suffered from the humiliation....

SORIN. And, by the way, can you tell me, please, what sort of man this literary gentleman is? There's no making him out. He never says anything.

TREPLEV. He is an intelligent man, good-natured and rather melancholy, you know. A very decent fellow. He is still a good distance off forty, but he is already celebrated and has enough and to spare of everything. As for his writings ... what shall I say? They are charming, full of talent, but ... after Tolstoy or Zola you do not care to read Trigorin.

SORIN. Well, I am fond of authors, my boy. At one time I had a passionate desire for two things: I wanted to get married, and I wanted to become an author; but I did not succeed in doing either. Yes, it is pleasant to be even a small author, as a matter of fact.

TREPLEV (*listens*). I hear steps ... (*embraces his uncle*). I cannot live without her.... The very sound of her footsteps is lovely.... I am wildly happy (*goes quickly to meet* NINA ZARETCHNY *as she enters*). My enchantress—my dream....

NINA (*in agitation*). I am not late.... Of course I am not late....

TREPLEV (*kissing her hands*). No, no, no!

NINA. I have been uneasy all day. I was so frightened. I was afraid father would not let me come.... But he has just gone out with my stepmother. The sky is red, the moon is just rising, and I kept urging on the horse (*laughs*). But I am glad (*shakes* SORIN's *hand warmly*).

SORIN (*laughs*). Your eyes look as though you have been crying.... Fie, fie! That's not right!

NINA. Oh, it was nothing.... You see how out of breath I am. I have to go in half an hour. We must make haste. I can't stay, I can't! For God's sake don't keep me! My father doesn't know I am here.

TREPLEV. It really is time to begin. We must go and call the others.

SORIN. I'll go this minute (*goes to the right, singing* "To France two grenadiers." *Looks round.*) Once I sang like that, and a deputy prosecutor said to me, "You have a powerful voice, your Excellency"; then he thought a little and added, "but not a pleasant one" (*laughs and goes off*).

NINA. My father and his wife won't let me come here. They say it is so Bohemian here ... they are afraid I shall go on the stage.... But I feel drawn to the lake here like a sea-gull.... My heart is full of you (*looks round*).

TREPLEV. We are alone.

NINA. I fancy there is someone there.

TREPLEV. There's nobody. (*They kiss.*)

NINA. What tree is this?

TREPLEV. An elm.

NINA. Why is it so dark?

TREPLEV. It's evening; everything is getting dark. Don't go away early, I entreat you!

NINA. I must.

TREPLEV. And if I come to you, Nina, I'll stand in the garden all night, watching your window.

NINA. You can't; the watchman would notice you. Trésor is not used to you, and he would bark.

TREPLEV. I love you!

NINA. Sh-h....

TREPLEV (*hearing footsteps*). Who is there? You, Yakov?

YAKOV (*behind the stage*). Yes, sir.

TREPLEV. Take your places. It's time to begin. Is the moon rising?

YAKOV. Yes, sir.

TREPLEV. Have you got the methylated spirit? Have you got the sulphur? When the red eyes appear there must be a smell of sulphur. (*To* NINA) Go, it's all ready. Are you nervous?

NINA. Yes, awfully! Your mother is all right—I am not afraid of her—but there's Trigorin ... I feel frightened and ashamed of acting before him ... a celebrated author.... Is he young?

TREPLEV. Yes.

NINA. How wonderful his stories are.

TREPLEV (*coldly*). I don't know. I haven't read them.

NINA. It is difficult to act in your play. There are no living characters in it.

TREPLEV. Living characters! One must depict life not as it is, and not as it ought to be, but as we see it in our dreams.

NINA. There is very little action in your play—nothing but speeches. And to my mind there ought to be love in a play. (*Both go behind the stage.*)

(*Enter* POLINA ANDREYEVNA *and* DORN.)

POLINA. It is getting damp. Go back and put on your goloshes.

DORN. I am hot.

POLINA. You don't take care of yourself. It's obstinacy. You are a doctor, and you know perfectly well that damp air is bad for you, but you want to make me miserable; you sat out on the verandah all yesterday evening on purpose....

DORN (*hums*). "Do not say that youth is ruined."

POLINA. You were so absorbed in conversation with Irina Nikolayevna ... you did not notice the cold. Own up ... you are attracted by her.

DORN. I am fifty-five.

POLINA. Nonsense! That's not old for a man. You look very young for your age, and are still attractive to women.

DORN. Well, what would you have?

POLINA. All you men are ready to fall down and worship an actress, all of you!

DORN (*hums*). "Before thee once again I stand." If artists are liked in society and treated differently from merchants, for example, that's only in the nature of things. It's idealism.

POLINA. Women have always fallen in love with you and thrown themselves on your neck. Is that idealism too?

DORN (*shrugs his shoulders*). Well, in the attitude of women to me there has been a great deal that was good. What they principally loved in me was a first-rate doctor. You remember that ten or fifteen years ago I was the only decent accoucheur in the district. Then, too, I have always been an honest man.

POLINA (*seizes him by the hand*). Dearest!

DORN. Sh-h! They are coming.

(*Enter* MADAME ARKADIN *arm in arm with* SORIN, TRIGORIN, SHAMRAEV, MEDVEDENKO *and* MASHA.)

SHAMRAEV. In the year 1873 she acted marvellously at the fair at Poltava. It was a delight! She acted exquisitely! Do you happen to know, madam, where Pavel Semyonitch Tchadin, a comic actor, is now? His Rasplyuev was inimitable, even finer than Sadovsky's, I assure you, honoured lady. Where is he now?

MADAME ARKADIN. You keep asking me about antediluvians. How should I know? (*Sits down.*)

SHAMRAEV (*with a sigh*). Pashka Tchadin! There are no such actors now. The stage has gone down, Irina Nikolayevna! In old days there were mighty oaks, but now we see nothing but stumps.

DORN. There are few actors of brilliant talents nowadays, that's true; but the average level of acting is far higher than it was.

SHAMRAEV. I can't agree with you. But, of course, it's a matter of taste. *De gustibus aut bene aut nihil.*

(TREPLEV *comes out from behind the stage.*)

MADAME ARKADIN (*to her son*). My dear son, when is it going to begin?

TREPLEV. In a minute. I beg you to be patient.

MADAME ARKADIN (*recites from* "Hamlet").

"Oh, Hamlet, speak no more!
 Thou turn'st mine eyes into my very soul;
 And there I see such black and grained spots
 As will not leave their tinct."

TREPLEV (*from* "Hamlet").

"And let me wring your heart, for so I shall,
 If it be made of penetrable stuff."

(*A horn is sounded behind the stage.*)

TREPLEV. Ladies and gentlemen, we begin! I beg you to attend (*a pause*). I begin (*taps with a stick and recites aloud*). Oh, you venerable

old shadows that float at nighttime over this lake, lull us to sleep
and let us dream of what will be in two hundred thousand years!

SORIN. There will be nothing in two hundred thousand years.

TREPLEV. Then let them present that nothing to us.

MADAME ARKADIN. Let them. We are asleep.

(*The curtain rises; the view of the lake is revealed; the moon is above the horizon, its reflection in the water; NINA ZARETCHNY, all in white, is sitting on a big stone.*)

NINA. Men, lions, eagles and partridges, horned deer, geese, spiders,
silent fish that dwell in the water, starfishes and creatures which
cannot be seen by the eye—all living things, all living things, all living things, having completed their cycle of sorrow, are extinct....
For thousands of years the earth has borne no living creature on its
surface, and this poor moon lights its lamp in vain. On the meadow
the cranes no longer waken with a cry, and there is no sound of the
May beetles in the lime trees. It is cold, cold, cold! Empty, empty,
empty! Dreadful, dreadful, dreadful! (*a pause*). The bodies of living
creatures have vanished into dust, and eternal matter has transformed them into rocks, into water, into clouds, while the souls
of all have melted into one. That world-soul I am—I.... In me is
the soul of Alexander the Great, of Cæsar, of Shakespeare and of
Napoleon, and of the lowest leech. In me the consciousness of men
is blended with the instincts of the animals, and I remember all, all,
all! And I live through every life over again in myself! (*Will-of-the-wisps appear.*)

MADAME ARKADIN (*softly*). It's something decadent.

TREPLEV (*in an imploring and reproachful voice*). Mother!

NINA. I am alone. Once in a hundred years I open my lips to speak,
and my voice echoes mournfully in the void, and no one hears....
You too, pale lights, hear me not.... The stagnant marsh begets you
before daybreak and you wander until dawn, but without thought,
without will, without the tremor of life. For fear that life should
spring up in you the father of eternal matter, the devil, keeps the
atoms in you, as in the stones and in the water, in continual flux, and
you are changing perpetually. For in all the universe nothing re-

mains permanent and unchanged but the spirit (*a pause*). Like a prisoner cast into a deep, empty well I know not where I am and what awaits me. All is hidden from me but that in the cruel, persistent struggle with the devil—the principle of the forces of matter—I am destined to conquer, and, after that, matter and spirit will be blended in glorious harmony and the Kingdom of the Cosmic Will will come. But that will come only little by little, through long, long thousands of years when the moon and the bright Sirius and the earth are changed to dust.... Till then—terror, terror ... (*a pause; two red spots appear upon the background of the lake*). Here my powerful foe, the devil, is approaching. I see his dreadful crimson eyes....

MADAME ARKADIN. There's a smell of sulphur. Is that as it should be?

TREPLEV. Yes.

MADAME ARKADIN (*laughs*). Oh, it's a stage effect!

TREPLEV. Mother!

NINA. He is dreary without man—

POLINA (*to* DORN). You have taken your hat off. Put it on or you will catch cold.

MADAME ARKADIN. The doctor has taken his hat off to the devil, the father of eternal matter.

TREPLEV (*firing up, aloud*). The play is over! Enough! Curtain!

MADAME ARKADIN. What are you cross about?

TREPLEV. Enough! The curtain! Let down the curtain! (*stamping*). Curtain! (*The curtain falls.*) I am sorry! I lost sight of the fact that only a few of the elect may write plays and act in them. I have infringed the monopoly. I ... I ... (*Tries to say something more, but with a wave of his hand goes out on left.*)

MADAME ARKADIN. What's the matter with him?

SORIN. Irina, you really must have more consideration for youthful vanity, my dear.

MADAME ARKADIN. What did I say to him?

SORIN. You hurt his feelings.

MADAME ARKADIN. He told us beforehand that it was a joke, and I regarded his play as a joke.

SORIN. All the same ...

MADAME ARKADIN. Now it appears that he has written a great work. What next! So he has got up this performance and smothered us with sulphur not as a joke but as a protest.... He wanted to show us how to write and what to act. This is getting tiresome! These continual sallies at my expense—these continual pin-pricks would put anyone out of patience, say what you like. He is a vain, whimsical boy!

SORIN. He meant to give you pleasure.

MADAME ARKADIN. Really? He did not choose an ordinary play, however, but made us listen to this decadent delirium. For the sake of a joke I am ready to listen to delirium, but here we have pretensions to new forms and a new view of art. To my thinking it's no question of new forms at all, but simply bad temper.

TRIGORIN. Everyone writes as he likes and as he can.

MADAME ARKADIN. Let him write as he likes and as he can, only let him leave me in peace.

DORN. Jupiter! you are angry....

MADAME ARKADIN. I am not Jupiter—I am a woman (*lights a cigarette*). I am not angry—I am only vexed that a young man should spend his time so drearily. I did not mean to hurt his feelings.

MEDVEDENKO. No one has any grounds to separate spirit from matter, seeing that spirit itself may be a combination of material atoms. (*With animation, to* TRIGORIN) But you know someone ought to write a play on how we poor teachers live, and get it acted. We have a hard, hard life.

MADAME ARKADIN. That's true, but don't let us talk either of plays or of atoms. It is such a glorious evening! Do you hear? There is singing! (*listens*). How nice it is!

POLINA. It's on the other side of the lake (*a pause*).

MADAME ARKADIN (*to* TRIGORIN). Sit down beside me. Ten or fifteen years ago there were sounds of music and singing on that lake continually almost every night. There are six country houses on the shores of the lake. I remember laughter, noise, shooting, and love affairs without end.... The *jeune premier* and the idol of all those six households was in those days our friend here, the doctor (*motions with her head towards* DORN), Yevgeny Sergeitch. He is fascinating still, but in those days he was irresistible. But my conscience is beginning to trouble me. Why did I hurt my poor boy's feelings? I feel worried. (*Aloud*) Kostya! Son! Kostya!

MASHA. I'll go and look for him.

MADAME ARKADIN. Please do, my dear.

MASHA (*going to the left*). Aa-oo! Konstantin Gavrilitch! Aa-oo! (*goes off*).

NINA (*coming out from behind the stage*). Apparently there will be no going on, and I may come out. Good evening! (*Kisses* MADAME ARKADIN *and* POLINA ANDREYEVNA.)

SORIN. Bravo! Bravo!

MADAME ARKADIN. Bravo! Bravo! We admired you. With such an appearance, with such a lovely voice, you really cannot stay in the country; it is a sin. You must have talent. Do you hear? It's your duty to go on the stage.

NINA. Oh, that's my dream! (*sighing*) But it will never be realised.

MADAME ARKADIN. Who knows? Here, let me introduce Boris Alexeyevitch Trigorin.

NINA. Oh, I am so glad ... (*overcome with embarrassment*). I am always reading your ...

MADAME ARKADIN (*making her sit down beside them*). Don't be shy, my dear. He is a celebrity, but he has a simple heart. You see, he is shy himself.

DORN. I suppose we may raise the curtain; it's rather uncanny.

SHAMRAEV (*aloud*). Yakov, pull up the curtain, my lad. (*The curtain goes up.*)

NINA (*to* TRIGORIN). It is a queer play, isn't it?

TRIGORIN. I did not understand it at all. But I enjoyed it. You acted so genuinely. And the scenery was delightful (*a pause*). There must be a lot of fish in that lake.

NINA. Yes.

TRIGORIN. I love angling. There is nothing I enjoy so much as sitting on the bank of a river in the evening and watching the float.

NINA. But I should have thought that for anyone who has known the enjoyment of creation, no other enjoyment can exist.

MADAME ARKADIN (*laughing*). Don't talk like that. When people say nice things to him he is utterly floored.

SHAMRAEV. I remember one evening in the opera theatre in Moscow the celebrated Silva took the lower *C!* As it happened, there was sitting in the gallery the bass of our church choir, and all at once—imagine our intense astonishment—we heard from the gallery "Bravo, Silva!" a whole octave lower—like this: (*in a deep bass*) "Bravo, Silva!" The audience sat spellbound (*a pause*).

DORN. The angel of silence has flown over us.

NINA. It's time for me to go. Good-bye.

MADAME ARKADIN. Where are you off to? Why so early? We won't let you go.

NINA. My father expects me.

MADAME ARKADIN. What a man, really ... (*kisses her*). Well, there is no help for it. I am sorry—I am sorry to let you go.

NINA. If you knew how grieved I am to go.

MADAME ARKADIN. Someone ought to see you home, my little dear.

NINA (*frightened*). Oh, no, no!

SORIN (*to her, in an imploring voice*). Do stay!

NINA. I can't, Pyotr Nikolayevitch.

SORIN. Stay for an hour. What is there in that?

NINA (*thinking a minute, tearfully*). I can't! (*Shakes hands and hurriedly goes off.*)

MADAME ARKADIN. Unfortunate girl she is, really. They say her mother left her father all her immense property—every farthing of it—and now the girl has got nothing, as her father has already made a will leaving everything to his second wife. It's monstrous!

DORN. Yes, her father is a pretty thorough scoundrel, one must do him the justice to say so.

SORIN (*rubbing his cold hands*). Let us go too, it's getting damp. My legs ache.

MADAME ARKADIN. They seem like wooden legs, you can hardly walk. Let us go, unlucky old man! (*Takes his arm.*)

SHAMRAEV (*offering his arm to his wife*). Madame?

SORIN. I hear that dog howling again. (*To* SHAMRAEV) Be so kind, Ilya Afanasyitch, as to tell them to let it off the chain.

SHAMRAEV. It's impossible, Pyotr Nikolayevitch, I am afraid of thieves getting into the barn. Our millet is there. (*To* MEDVEDENKO, *who is walking beside him*) Yes, a whole octave lower: "Bravo, Silva!" And he not a singer—simply a church chorister!

MEDVEDENKO. And what salary does a chorister get? (*All go out except* DORN.)

DORN (*alone*). I don't know, perhaps I know nothing about it, or have gone off my head, but I liked the play. There is something in it. When that girl talked about loneliness and afterwards when the devil's eyes appeared, I was so excited that my hands trembled. It is fresh, naïve.... Here he comes, I believe. I want to say all the nice things I can to him.

TREPLEV (*enters*). They have all gone.

DORN. I am here.

TREPLEV. Mashenka is looking for me all over the park. Insufferable creature she is!

DORN. Konstantin Gavrilitch, I liked your play extremely. It's a strange thing, and I haven't heard the end, and yet it made a strong impression! You are a gifted man—you must persevere.

(TREPLEV *presses his hand warmly and embraces him impulsively.*)

DORN. Fie, what an hysterical fellow! There are tears in his eyes! What I mean is this. You have taken a subject from the realm of abstract ideas. So it should be, for a work of art ought to express a great idea. A thing is only fine when it is serious. How pale you are!

TREPLEV. So you tell me to persevere?

DORN. Yes.... But write only of what is important and eternal. You know, I have had varied experiences of life, and have enjoyed it; I am satisfied, but if it had been my lot to know the spiritual heights which artists reach at the moment of creation, I should, I believe, have despised my bodily self and all that appertains to it and left all things earthly as far behind as possible.

TREPLEV. Excuse me, where is Nina?

DORN. And another thing. In a work of art there ought to be a clear definite idea. You ought to know what is your aim in writing, for if you go along that picturesque route without a definite goal you will be lost and your talent will be your ruin.

TREPLEV (*impatiently*). Where is Nina?

DORN. She has gone home.

TREPLEV (*in despair*). What am I to do? I want to see her ... I must see her.... I must go....

(*Enter* MASHA.)

DORN (*to* TREPLEV). Calm yourself, my boy.

TREPLEV. But I am going all the same. I must go.

MASHA. Come indoors, Konstantin Gavrilitch. Your mother wants you. She is worried.

TREPLEV. Tell her that I have gone away. And I beg you—all of you— leave me in peace! Let me alone! Don't follow me about!

DORN. Come, come, come, dear boy.... You can't go on like that.... That's not the thing.

TREPLEV (*in tears*). Good-bye, doctor. Thank you ... (*goes off*).

DORN (*with a sigh*). Youth! youth!

MASHA. When people have nothing better to say, they say, "Youth! youth!" ... (*Takes a pinch of snuff.*)

DORN (*takes her snuff-box from her and flings it into the bushes*). That's disgusting! (*a pause*). I believe they are playing the piano indoors. We must go in.

MASHA. Wait a little.

DORN. What is it?

MASHA. I want to tell you once more. I have a longing to talk ... (*growing agitated*). I don't care for my father ... but I feel drawn to you. For some reason I feel with all my heart that you are very near me.... Help me. Help me, or I shall do something silly, I shall make a mock of my life and ruin it.... I can't go on....

DORN. What is it? Help you in what?

MASHA. I am miserable. No one, no one knows how miserable I am! (*Laying her head on his breast, softly*) I love Konstantin!

DORN. How hysterical they all are! How hysterical! And what a lot of love.... Oh, the sorcery of the lake! (*Tenderly*) But what can I do, my child? What? What?

CURTAIN.

ACT II

A croquet lawn. The house with a big verandah in the background on the right, on the left is seen the lake with the blazing sun reflected in it.

Flower beds. Midday. Hot. MADAME ARKADIN, DORN *and* MASHA *are sitting on a garden seat in the shade of an old lime tree on one side of the croquet lawn.* DORN *has an open book on his knee.*

MADAME ARKADIN (*to* MASHA). Come, let us stand up. (*They both get up.*) Let us stand side by side. You are twenty-two and I am nearly twice as old. Yevgeny Sergeitch, which of us looks the younger?

DORN. You, of course.

MADAME ARKADIN. There! And why is it? Because I work, I feel I am always on the go, while you stay always in the same place and have no life at all.... And it is my rule never to look into the future. I never think about old age or death. What is to be, will be.

MASHA. And I feel as though I had been born long, long ago; I trail my life along like an endless train.... And often I have not the slightest desire to go on living (*sits down*). Of course, that's all nonsense. I must shake myself and throw it all off.

DORN (*hums quietly*). "Tell her, my flowers."

MADAME ARKADIN. Then I am as particular as an Englishman. I keep myself in hand, as they say, my dear, and am always dressed and have my hair done *comme il faut*. Do I allow myself to go out of the house even into the garden in a dressing-gown, or without my hair being done? Never! What has preserved me is that I have never been a dowdy, I have never let myself go, as some women do ... (*walks about the lawn with her arms akimbo*). Here I am, as brisk as a bird. I could take the part of a girl of fifteen.

DORN. Nevertheless, I shall go on (*takes up the book*). We stopped at the corn merchant and the rats....

MADAME ARKADIN. And the rats. Read (*sits down*). But give it to me, I'll read. It is my turn (*takes the book and looks in it*). And rats.... Here it is.... (*Reads*) "And of course for society people to spoil novelists and to attract them to themselves is as dangerous as for a corn merchant to rear rats in his granaries. And yet they love them. And so, when a woman has picked out an author whom she desires to captivate, she lays siege to him by means of compliments, flattery and favours..." Well, that may be so with the French, but there is nothing like that with us, we have no set rules. Among us, before a woman sets to work to captivate an author, she is generally head over ears in love herself, if you please. To go no further, take Trigorin and me....

(*Enter* SORIN, *leaning on his stick and with him* NINA; MEDVEDENKO *wheels an empty bath-chair in after them.*)

SORIN (*in a caressing tone, as to a child*). Yes? We are delighted, aren't we? We are happy to-day at last? (*To his sister*) We are delighted! Our father and stepmother have gone off to Tver, and we are free now for three whole days.

NINA (*sits down beside* MADAME ARKADIN *and embraces her*). I am happy! Now I belong to you.

SORIN (*sits down in his bath-chair*). She looks quite a beauty to-day.

MADAME ARKADIN. Nicely dressed and interesting.... That's a good girl (*kisses* NINA). But we mustn't praise you too much for fear of ill-luck. Where is Boris Alexeyevitch?

NINA. He is in the bathing-house, fishing.

MADAME ARKADIN. I wonder he doesn't get sick of it! (*is about to go on reading*).

NINA. What is that?

MADAME ARKADIN. Maupassant's "Sur l'eau," my dear (*reads a few lines to herself*). Well, the rest isn't interesting or true (*shuts the book*). I feel uneasy. Tell me, what's wrong with my son? Why is he so depressed and ill-humoured? He spends whole days on the lake and I hardly ever see him.

MASHA. His heart is troubled. (*To* NINA, *timidly*) Please, do read us something out of his play!

NINA (*shrugging her shoulders*). Would you like it? It's so uninteresting.

MASHA (*restraining her enthusiasm*). When he reads anything himself his eyes glow and his face turns pale. He has a fine mournful voice, and the gestures of a poet.

(*There is a sound of* SORIN *snoring.*)

DORN. Good night!

MADAME ARKADIN. Petrusha!

SORIN. Ah?

MADAME ARKADIN. Are you asleep?

SORIN. Not a bit of it (*a pause*).

MADAME ARKADIN. You do nothing for your health, brother, and that's not right.

SORIN. I should like to take something, but the doctor won't give me anything.

DORN. Take medicine at sixty!

SORIN. Even at sixty one wants to live!

DORN (*with vexation*). Oh, very well, take valerian drops!

MADAME ARKADIN. It seems to me it would do him good to go to some mineral springs.

DORN. Well, he might go. And he might not.

MADAME ARKADIN. What is one to make of that?

DORN. There's nothing to make of it. It's quite clear (*a pause*).

MEDVEDENKO. Pyotr Nikolayevitch ought to give up smoking.

SORIN. Nonsense!

DORN. No, it's not nonsense. Wine and tobacco destroy the personality. After a cigar or a glass of vodka, you are not Pyotr Nikolayevitch any more but Pyotr Nikolayevitch plus somebody else; your ego is diffused and you feel towards yourself as to a third person.

SORIN (*laughs*). It's all very well for you to argue! You've lived your life, but what about me? I have served in the Department of Justice for twenty-eight years, but I haven't lived yet, I've seen and done nothing as a matter of fact, and very naturally I want to live very much. You've had enough and you don't care, and so you are inclined to be philosophical, but I want to live, and so I drink sherry at dinner and smoke cigars and so on. That's all it comes to.

DORN. One must look at life seriously, but to go in for cures at sixty and to regret that one hasn't enjoyed oneself enough in one's youth is frivolous, if you will forgive my saying so.

MASHA (*gets up*). It must be lunch-time (*walks with a lazy, lagging step*). My leg is gone to sleep (*goes off*).

DORN. She will go and have a couple of glasses before lunch.

SORIN. She has no personal happiness, poor thing.

DORN. Nonsense, your Excellency.

SORIN. You argue like a man who has had all he wants.

MADAME ARKADIN. Oh, what can be more boring than this sweet country boredom! Hot, still, no one ever doing anything, everyone airing their theories.... It's nice being with you, my friends, charming to listen to you, but ... to sit in a hotel room somewhere and learn one's part is ever so much better.

NINA (*enthusiastically*). Delightful! I understand you.

SORIN. Of course, it's better in town. You sit in your study, the footman lets no one in unannounced, there's a telephone ... in the streets there are cabs and everything....

DORN (*hums*). "Tell her, my flowers."

(*Enter* SHAMRAEV, *and after him* POLINA ANDREYEVNA).

SHAMRAEV. Here they are! Good morning! (*kisses* MADAME ARKADIN'S *hand and then* NINA'S). Delighted to see you in good health. (*To* MADAME ARKADIN) My wife tells me that you are proposing to drive into town with her to-day. Is that so?

MADAME ARKADIN. Yes, we are thinking of it.

SHAMRAEV. Hm! that's splendid, but how are you going, honoured lady? They are carting the rye to-day; all the men are at work. What horses are you to have, allow me to ask?

MADAME AKRADIN. What horses? How can I tell which?

SORIN. We've got carriage horses.

SHAMRAEV (*growing excited*). Carriage horses! But where am I to get collars for them? Where am I to get collars? It's a strange thing! It passes my understanding! Honoured lady! forgive me, I am full of reverence for your talent. I would give ten years of my life for you, but I cannot let you have the horses!

MADAME ARKADIN. But if I have to go! It's a queer thing!

SHAMRAEV. Honoured lady! you don't know what farming means.

MADAME ARKADIN (*flaring up*). That's the old story! If that's so, I go back to Moscow to-day. Give orders for horses to be hired for me at the village, or I'll walk to the station.

SHAMRAEV (*flaring up*). In that case I resign my position! You must look for another steward (*goes off*).

MADAME ARKADIN. It's like this every summer; every summer I am insulted here! I won't set my foot in the place again (*goes off at left where the bathing shed is supposed to be; a minute later she can be seen entering the house.* TRIGORIN *follows her, carrying fishing rods and tackle, and a pail*).

SORIN (*flaring up*). This is insolence! It's beyond everything. I am thoroughly sick of it. Send all the horses here this minute!

NINA (*to* POLINA ANDREYEVNA). To refuse Irina Nikolayevna, the famous actress! Any wish of hers, any whim even, is of more consequence than all your farming. It's positively incredible!

POLINA (*in despair*). What can I do? Put yourself in my position: what can I do?

SORIN (*to* NINA). Let us go to my sister. We will all entreat her not to go away. Won't we? (*Looking in the direction in which* SHAMRAEV *has gone*) Insufferable man! Despot!

NINA (*preventing him from getting up*). Sit still, sit still. We will wheel you in. (*She and* MEDVEDENKO *push the bath-chair.*) Oh, how awful it is!

SORIN. Yes, yes, it's awful. But he won't leave, I'll speak to him directly. (*They go out;* DORN *and* POLINA ANDREYEVNA *are left alone on the stage.*)

DORN. People are tiresome. Your husband ought to be simply kicked out, but it will end in that old woman Pyotr Nikolayevitch and his sister begging the man's pardon. You will see!

POLINA. He has sent the carriage horses into the fields too! And there are misunderstandings like this every day. If you only knew how it upsets me! It makes me ill; see how I am trembling.... I can't endure his rudeness. (*In an imploring voice*) Yevgeny, dearest, light of my eyes, my darling, let me come to you.... Our time is passing, we are no longer young, and if only we could lay aside concealment and lying for the end of our lives, anyway ... (*a pause*).

DORN. I am fifty-five; it's too late to change my life.

POLINA. I know you refuse me because there are other women too who are as near to you. You can't take them all to live with you. I understand. Forgive me, you are tired of me.

(NINA *appears near the house; she is picking flowers.*)

DORN. No, it's all right.

POLINA. I am wretched from jealousy. Of course you are a doctor, you can't avoid women. I understand.

DORN (*to* NINA, *who comes up to them*). How are things going?

NINA. Irina Nikolayevna is crying and Pyotr Nikolayevitch has an attack of asthma.

DORN (*gets up*). I'd better go and give them both valerian drops.

NINA (*gives him the flowers*). Please take these.

DORN. *Merci bien* (*goes towards the house*).

POLINA (*going with him*). What charming flowers! (*Near the house, in a smothered voice*) Give me those flowers! Give me those flowers! (*On receiving them tears the flowers to pieces and throws them away; both go into the house.*)

NINA (*alone*). How strange it is to see a famous actress cry, and about such a trivial thing! And isn't it strange? A famous author, adored by the public, written about in all the papers, his photographs for sale, his works translated into foreign languages—and he spends the whole day fishing and is delighted that he has caught two gudgeon. I thought famous people were proud, unapproachable, that they despised the crowd, and by their fame and the glory of their name, as it were, revenged themselves on the vulgar herd for putting rank and wealth above everything. But here they cry and fish, play cards, laugh and get cross like everyone else!

TREPLEV (*comes in without a hat on, with a gun and a dead sea-gull*). Are you alone here?

NINA. Yes.

(TREPLEV *lays the sea-gull at her feet.*)

NINA. What does that mean?

TREPLEV. I was so mean as to kill this bird to-day. I lay it at your feet.

NINA. What is the matter with you? (*Picks up the bird and looks at it.*)

TREPLEV (*after a pause*). Soon I shall kill myself in the same way.

NINA. You have so changed, I hardly know you.

TREPLEV. Yes, ever since the day when I hardly knew you. You have changed to me, your eyes are cold, you feel me in the way.

NINA. You have become irritable of late, you express yourself so incomprehensibly, as it were in symbols. This bird is a symbol too, I suppose, but forgive me, I don't understand it (*lays the sea-gull on the seat*). I am too simple to understand you.

TREPLEV. This began from that evening when my play came to grief so stupidly. Women never forgive failure. I have burnt it all; every scrap of it. If only you knew how miserable I am! Your growing cold to me is awful, incredible, as though I had woken up and found this lake had suddenly dried up or sunk into the earth. You have just said that you are too simple to understand me. Oh, what is there to understand? My play was not liked, you despise my inspiration, you already consider me commonplace, insignificant, like so many others ... (*stamping*). How well I understand it all, how I understand it! I feel as though I had a nail in my brain, damnation take it together with my vanity which is sucking away my life, sucking it like a snake ... (*sees* TRIGORIN, *who comes in reading a book*). Here comes the real genius, walking like Hamlet and with a book too. (*Mimics*) "Words, words, words." ... The sun has scarcely reached you and you are smiling already, your eyes are melting in its rays. I won't be in your way (*goes off quickly*).

TRIGORIN (*making notes in his book*). Takes snuff and drinks vodka. Always in black. The schoolmaster is in love with her....

NINA. Good morning, Boris Alexeyevitch!

TRIGORIN. Good morning. Circumstances have turned out so unexpectedly that it seems we are setting off to-day. We are hardly likely to meet again. I am sorry. I don't often have the chance of meeting young girls, youthful and charming; I have forgotten how one feels at eighteen or nineteen and can't picture it to myself, and so the young girls in my stories and novels are usually false. I should like to be in your shoes just for one hour to find out how you think, and altogether what sort of person you are.

NINA. And I should like to be in your shoes.

TRIGORIN. What for?

NINA. To know what it feels like to be a famous, gifted author.

What does it feel like to be famous? How does it affect you, being famous?

TRIGORIN. How? Nohow, I believe. I have never thought about it. (*After a moment's thought*) It's one of two things: either you exaggerate my fame, or it never is felt at all.

NINA. But if you read about yourself in the newspapers?

TRIGORIN. When they praise me I am pleased, and when they abuse me I feel out of humour for a day or two.

NINA. What a wonderful world! If only you knew how I envy you! How different people's lots in life are! Some can scarcely get through their dull, obscure existence, they are all just like one another, they are all unhappy; while others—you, for instance—you are one out of a million, have an interesting life full of brightness and significance. You are happy.

TRIGORIN. I? (*shrugging his shoulders*) Hm.... You talk of fame and happiness, of bright interesting life, but to me all those fine words, if you will forgive my saying so, are just like a sweetmeat which I never taste. You are very young and very good-natured.

NINA. Your life is splendid!

TRIGORIN. What is there particularly nice in it? (*Looks at his watch*) I must go and write directly. Excuse me, I mustn't stay ... (*laughs*). You have stepped on my favourite corn, as the saying is, and here I am beginning to get excited and a little cross. Let us talk though. We will talk about my splendid bright life.... Well, where shall we begin? (*After thinking a little*) There are such things as fixed ideas, when a man thinks day and night, for instance, of nothing but the moon. And I have just such a moon. I am haunted day and night by one persistent thought: I ought to be writing, I ought to be writing, I ought... I have scarcely finished one novel when, for some reason, I must begin writing another, then a third, after the third a fourth. I write incessantly, post haste, and I can't write in any other way. What is there splendid and bright in that, I ask you? Oh, it's an absurd life! Here I am with you; I am excited, yet every moment I remember that my unfinished novel is waiting for me. Here I see a cloud that looks like a grand piano. I think that I must put into a story somewhere that a cloud sailed by that looked like a grand piano. There is a scent of heliotrope. I hurriedly make a note: a sickly smell, a widow's flower, to be mentioned in the description of a summer evening. I catch up myself and you at every sentence, every word, and make haste to put those sentences and words away into my literary treasure-house—it may come in useful! When I finish work I race off to the theatre or to fishing; if only I could rest in that and forget myself. But no, there's a new subject rolling about in my head like a heavy iron cannon ball, and I am drawn to my writing table and must make haste again to go on writing and writing. And it's always like that, always. And I have no rest from myself, and I feel that I am eating up my own life, and that for the sake of the honey I give to someone in space I am stripping the pollen from my best flowers, tearing up the flowers themselves and trampling on their roots. Don't you think I am mad? Do my friends and acquaintances treat me as though I were sane? "What are you writing? What are you giving us?" It's the same thing again and again, and it seems to me as though my friends' notice, their praises, their enthusiasm—that it's all a sham, that they are deceiving me as an invalid and I am somehow afraid that they will steal up to me from behind, snatch me and carry me off and put me in a mad-house. And in those years, the best years of my youth, when I was beginning, my writing was unmixed torture. A small writer, particularly when he is not successful, seems to himself clumsy, awkward, unnecessary; his nerves are strained and overwrought. He can't resist hanging about people connected with literature and art, unrecognised and unnoticed by anyone, afraid to look anyone boldly in the face, like a passionate gambler without any money. I hadn't seen my reader, but for some reason I always imagined him hostile, and mistrustful. I was afraid of the public, it alarmed me, and when I had to produce my first play it always seemed to me that all the dark people felt hostile and all the fair ones were coldly indifferent. Oh, how awful it was! What agony it was!

NINA. But surely inspiration and the very process of creation give you moments of exalted happiness?

TRIGORIN. Yes. While I am writing I enjoy it. And I like reading my proofs, but ... as soon as it is published I can't endure it, and I see that it is all wrong, a mistake, that it ought not to have been written at all, and I feel vexed and sick about it ... (*laughing*). And the public reads it and says: "Yes, charming, clever. Charming, but very inferior to Tolstoy," or, "It's a fine thing, but Turgenev's 'Fathers and Children' is finer." And it will be the same to my dying day, only charming and clever, charming and clever—and nothing more. And when I die my friends, passing by my tomb, will say, "Here lies Trigorin. He was a good writer, but inferior to Turgenev."

NINA. Forgive me, but I refuse to understand you. You are simply spoiled by success.

TRIGORIN. What success? I have never liked myself; I dislike my own work. The worst of it is that I am in a sort of delirium, and often don't understand what I am writing. I love this water here, the trees, the sky. I feel nature, it arouses in me a passionate, irresistible desire to write. But I am not simply a landscape painter; I am also a citizen. I love my native country, my people; I feel that if I am a writer I am in duty bound to write of the people, of their sufferings, of their future, to talk about science and the rights of man and so on, and so on, and I write about everything. I am hurried and flustered, and on all sides they whip me up and are angry with me; I dash about from side to side like a fox beset by hounds. I see life and culture continually getting farther and farther away while I fall farther and farther behind like a peasant too late for the train; and what it comes to is that I feel I can only describe scenes and in everything else I am false to the marrow of my bones.

NINA. You are overworked and have not the leisure nor the desire to appreciate your own significance. You may be dissatisfied with yourself, but for others you are great and splendid! If I were a writer like you, I should give up my whole life to the common herd, but I should know that there could be no greater happiness for them than to rise to my level, and they would harness themselves to my chariot.

TRIGORIN. My chariot, what next! Am I an Agamemnon, or what? (*Both smile.*)

NINA. For such happiness as being a writer or an artist I would be ready to endure poverty, disappointment, the dislike of those around me; I would live in a garret and eat nothing but rye bread, I would suffer from being dissatisfied with myself, from recognising my own imperfections, but I should ask in return for fame ... real, resounding fame.... (*covers her face with her hands*). It makes me dizzy.... Ough!

(*The voice of* MADAME ARKADIN *from the house.*)

MADAME ARKADIN. Boris Alexeyevitch!

TRIGORIN. They are calling for me. I suppose it's to pack. But I don't want to leave here. (*Looks round at the lake.*) Just look how glorious it is! It's splendid!

NINA. Do you see the house and garden on the other side of the lake?

TRIGORIN. Yes.

NINA. That house was my dear mother's. I was born there. I have spent all my life beside this lake and I know every little islet on it.

TRIGORIN. It's very delightful here! (*Seeing the sea-gull*) And what's this?

NINA. A sea-gull. Konstantin Gavrilitch shot it.

TRIGORIN. A beautiful bird. Really, I don't want to go away. Try and persuade Irina Nikolayevna to stay (*makes a note in his book*).

NINA. What are you writing?

TRIGORIN. Oh, I am only making a note. A subject struck me (*putting away the note-book*). A subject for a short story: a young girl, such as you, has lived all her life beside a lake; she loves the lake like a sea-gull, and is as free and happy as a sea-gull. But a man comes by chance, sees her, and having nothing better to do, destroys her like that sea-gull here (*a pause*).

(MADAME ARKADIN *appears at the window.*)

MADAME ARKADIN. Boris Alexeyevitch, where are you?

TRIGORIN. I am coming (*goes and looks back at* NINA. *To* MADAME ARKADIN *at the window*). What is it?

MADAME ARKADIN. We are staying.

(TRIGORIN *goes into the house.*)

NINA (*advances to the footlights; after a few moments' meditation*) It's a dream!

CURTAIN.

ACT III

The dining-room in Sorin's *house. Doors on right and on left. A sideboard. A medicine cupboard. A table in the middle of the room. A portmanteau and hat-boxes; signs of preparation for departure.* Trigorin *is having lunch;* Masha *stands by the table.*

Masha. I tell all this to you as a writer. You may make use of it. I am telling you the truth: if he had hurt himself seriously I would not have gone on living another minute. But I have pluck enough all the same. I just made up my mind that I would tear this love out of my heart, tear it out by the roots.

Trigorin. How are you going to do that?

Masha. I am going to be married. To Medvedenko.

Trigorin. That's the schoolmaster?

Masha. Yes.

Trigorin. I don't understand what's the object of it.

Masha. To love without hope, to spend whole years waiting for something.... But when I marry, there will be no time left for love, new cares will smother all the old feelings. And, anyway, it will be a change, you know. Shall we have another?

Trigorin. Won't that be too much?

Masha. Oh, come! (*Fills two glasses*). Don't look at me like that! Women drink much oftener than you imagine. Only a small proportion drink openly as I do, the majority drink in secret. Yes. And it's always vodka or brandy. (*Clinks glasses*) My best wishes! You are a good-hearted man; I am sorry to be parting from you. (*They drink.*)

Trigorin. I don't want to go myself.

Masha. You should beg her to stay.

Trigorin. No, she won't stay now. Her son is behaving very tactlessly. First, he shoots himself, and now they say he is going to challenge me to a duel. And whatever for? He sulks, and snorts, and preaches new forms of art.... But there is room for all—new and old—why quarrel about it?

MASHA. Well, there's jealousy too. But it is nothing to do with me.

(*A pause.* YAKOV *crosses from right to left with a portmanteau.* NINA *enters and stands by the window.*)

MASHA. My schoolmaster is not very brilliant, but he is a good-natured man, and poor, and he is very much in love with me. I am sorry for him. And I am sorry for his old mother. Well, let me wish you all happiness. Don't remember evil against me (*shakes hands with him warmly*). I am very grateful for your friendly interest. Send me your books and be sure to put in an inscription. Only don't write, "To my honoured friend," but write simply, "To Marya, who belongs nowhere and has no object in life." Good-bye! (*Goes out.*)

NINA (*stretching out her arm towards* TRIGORIN, *with her fist clenched*). Odd or even?

TRIGORIN. Even.

NINA (*with a sigh*). Wrong. I had only one pea in my hand. I was trying my fortune whether to go on the stage or not. I wish someone would advise me.

TRIGORIN. It's impossible to advise in such a matter (*a pause*).

NINA. We are parting and ... perhaps we shall never meet again. Won't you please take this little medallion as a parting gift? I had your initials engraved on one side of it ... and on the other the title of your book, "Days and Nights."

TRIGORIN. How exquisite! (*kisses the medallion*). A charming present!

NINA. Think of me sometimes.

TRIGORIN. I shall think of you. I shall think of you as you were on that sunny day—do you remember?—a week ago, when you were wearing a light dress ... we were talking ... there was a white sea-gull lying on the seat.

NINA (*pensively*). Yes, a sea-gull ... (*a pause*). We can't talk any more, there's someone coming.... Let me have two minutes before you go, I entreat you ... (*goes out on the left*).

(*At the same instant* MADAME ARKADIN, SORIN *in a dress coat with a star of some order on it, then* YAKOV, *occupied with the luggage, enter on the right.*)

MADAME ARKADIN. Stay at home, old man. With your rheumatism you ought not to go gadding about. (*To* TRIGORIN) Who was that went out? Nina?

TRIGORIN. Yes.

MADAME ARKADIN. *Pardon,* we interrupted you (*sits down*). I believe I have packed everything. I am worn out.

TRIGORIN (*reads on the medallion*). " 'Days and Nights,' page 121, lines 11 and 12."

YAKOV (*clearing the table*). Am I to pack your fishing things too, sir?

TRIGORIN. Yes, I shall want them again. You can give away the hooks.

YAKOV. Yes, sir.

TRIGORIN (*to himself*). Page 121, lines 11 and 12. What is there in those lines? (*To* MADAME ARKADIN) Are there copies of my books in the house?

MADAME ARKADIN. Yes, in my brother's study, in the corner bookcase.

TRIGORIN. Page 121 ... (*goes out*).

MADAME ARKADIN. Really, Petrusha, you had better stay at home.

SORIN. You are going away; it will be dreary for me at home without you.

MADAME ARKADIN. And what is there in the town?

SORIN. Nothing particular, but still ... (*laughs*). There will be the laying of the foundation-stone of the Zemstvo-hall, and all that sort of thing. One longs to shake oneself free from this stagnant existence, if only for an hour or two. I've been too long on the shelf like some old cigarette-holder. I have ordered the horses for one o'clock; we'll set off at the same time.

MADAME ARKADIN (*after a pause*). Come, stay here, don't be bored and don't catch cold. Look after my son. Take care of him. Give him good advice (*a pause*). Here I am going away and I shall never know why Konstantin tried to shoot himself. I fancy jealousy was the chief cause, and the sooner I get Trigorin away from here, the better.

SORIN. What can I say? There were other reasons too. It's easy to understand; he is young, intelligent, living in the country, in the wilds, with no money, no position and no future. He has nothing to do. He is ashamed of his idleness and afraid of it. I am very fond of him indeed, and he is attached to me, yet in spite of it all he feels he is superfluous in the house, that he is a dependant, a poor relation. It's easy to understand, it's *amour propre....*

MADAME ARKADIN. He is a great anxiety to me! (*Pondering*) He might go into the service, perhaps.

SORIN (*begins to whistle, then irresolutely*). I think that quite the best thing would be if you were to ... let him have a little money. In the first place he ought to be able to be dressed like other people and all that. Just look at him, he's been going about in the same wretched jacket for the last three years and he has no overcoat ... (*laughs*). It would do him no harm to have a little fun ... to go abroad or something.... It wouldn't cost much.

MADAME ARKADIN. But all the same ... I might manage the suit, perhaps, but as for going abroad ... No, just at the moment I can't even manage the suit. (*Resolutely*) I have no money!

(SORIN *laughs.*)

MADAME ARKADIN. No!

SORIN (*begins to whistle*). Quite so. Forgive me, my dear, don't be cross. I believe you.... You are a generous, noble-hearted woman.

MADAME ARKADIN (*weeping*). I have no money.

SORIN. If I had money, of course I would give him some myself, but I have nothing, not a half-penny (*laughs*). My steward takes all my pension and spends it all on the land and the cattle and the bees, and my money is all wasted. The bees die, and the cows die, they never let me have horses....

MADAME ARKADIN. Yes, I have money, but you see I am an actress; my dresses alone are enough to ruin me.

SORIN. You are a kind, good creature ... I respect you.... Yes ... but there, I got a touch of it again ... (*staggers*). I feel dizzy (*clutches at the table*). I feel ill and all that.

MADAME ARKADIN (*alarmed*). Petrusha! (*trying to support him*). Petrusha, my dear! (*Calling*) Help! help!

(*Enter* TREPLEV *with a bandage round his head and* MEDVEDENKO.)

MADAME ARKADIN. He feels faint!

SORIN. It's all right, it's all right! (*Smiles and drinks some water*). It's passed off ... and all that.

TREPLEV (*to his mother*). Don't be frightened, Mother, it's not serious. Uncle often has these attacks now. (*To his uncle*) You must lie down, uncle.

SORIN. For a little while, yes.... But I am going to the town all the same.... I'll lie down a little and then set off.... It's quite natural (*goes out leaning on his stick*).

MEDVEDENKO (*gives him his arm*). There's a riddle: in the morning on four legs, at noon on two, in the evening on three....

SORIN (*laughs*). Just so. And at night on the back. Thank you, I can manage alone....

MEDVEDENKO. Oh come, why stand on ceremony! (*Goes out with* SORIN.)

MADAME ARKADIN. How he frightened me!

TREPLEV. It is not good for him to live in the country. He gets depressed. If you would be generous for once, Mother, and lend him fifteen hundred or two thousand roubles, he could spend a whole year in town.

MADAME ARKADIN. I have no money. I am an actress, not a banker (*a pause*).

TREPLEV. Mother, change my bandage. You do it so well.

MADAME ARKADIN (*takes out of the medicine cupboard some iodoform and a box with bandaging material*). The doctor is late.

TREPLEV. He promised to be here at ten, and it is midday already.

MADAME ARKADIN. Sit down (*takes the bandage off his head*). It's like a turban. Yesterday a stranger asked in the kitchen what nationality you were. But you have almost completely healed. There is the merest trifle left (*kisses him on the head*). You won't do anything naughty again while I am away, will you?

TREPLEV. No, Mother. It was a moment of mad despair when I could not control myself. It won't happen again. (*Kisses her hand*) You have such clever hands. I remember, long ago, when you were still acting at the Imperial Theatre—I was little then—there was a fight in our yard and a washerwoman, one of the tenants, was badly beaten. Do you remember? She was picked up senseless ... you looked after her, took her remedies and washed her children in a tub. Don't you remember?

MADAME ARKADIN. No (*puts on a fresh bandage*).

TREPLEV. Two ballet dancers lived in the same house as we did at the time.... They used to come to you and have coffee....

MADAME ARKADIN. I remember that.

TREPLEV. They were very pious (*a pause*). Just lately, these last days, I have loved you as tenderly and completely as when I was a child. I have no one left now but you. Only why, why do you give yourself up to the influence of that man?

MADAME ARKADIN. You don't understand him, Konstantin. He is a very noble character....

TREPLEV. And yet when he was told I was going to challenge him, the nobility of his character did not prevent him from funking it. He is going away. Ignominious flight!

MADAME ARKADIN. What nonsense! It is I who am asking him to go.

TREPLEV. A very noble character! Here you and I are almost quarrelling over him, and at this very moment he is somewhere in the drawing-room or the garden laughing at us ... developing Nina, trying to convince her finally that he is a genius.

MADAME ARKADIN. You take a pleasure in saying unpleasant things to me. I respect that man and beg you not to speak ill of him before me.

TREPLEV. And I don't respect him. You want me to think him a genius too, but forgive me, I can't tell lies, his books make me sick.

MADAME ARKADIN. That's envy. There's nothing left for people who have pretension without talent but to attack real talent. Much comfort in that, I must say!

TREPLEV (*ironically*). Real talent! (*Wrathfully*) I have more talent than all of you put together if it comes to that! (*Tears the bandage off his head*) You, with your hackneyed conventions, have usurped the supremacy in art and consider nothing real and legitimate but what you do yourselves; everything else you stifle and suppress. I don't believe in you! I don't believe in you or in him!

MADAME ARKADIN. Decadent!

TREPLEV. Get away to your charming theatre and act there in your paltry, stupid plays!

MADAME ARKADIN. I have never acted in such plays. Let me alone! You are not capable of writing even a wretched burlesque! You are nothing but a Kiev shopman! living on other people!

TREPLEV. You miser!

MADAME ARKADIN. You ragged beggar!

(TREPLEV *sits down and weeps quietly.*)

MADAME ARKADIN. Nonentity! (*Walking up and down in agitation*) Don't cry.... You mustn't cry (*weeps*). Don't ... (*kisses him on the forehead, on the cheeks and on the head*). My dear child, forgive me.... Forgive your sinful mother. Forgive me, you know I am wretched.

TREPLEV (*puts his arms round her*). If only you knew! I have lost everything! She does not love me, and now I cannot write ... all my hopes are gone....

MADAME ARKADIN. Don't despair ... Everything will come right. He is going away directly, she will love you again (*wipes away his tears*). Give over. We have made it up now.

TREPLEV (*kisses her hands*). Yes, Mother.

MADAME ARKADIN (*tenderly*). Make it up with him too. You don't want a duel, do you?

TREPLEV. Very well. Only, Mother, do allow me not to meet him. It's painful to me—it's more than I can bear. (*Enter* TRIGORIN.) Here he is ... I am going ... (*rapidly puts away the dressings in the cupboard*). The doctor will do the bandaging now.

TRIGORIN (*looking in a book*). Page 121 ... lines 11 and 12. Here it is. (*Reads*) "If ever my life can be of use to you, come and take it."

(TREPLEV *picks up the bandage from the floor and goes out.*)

MADAME ARKADIN (*looking at her watch*). The horses will soon be here.

TRIGORIN (*to himself*). "If ever my life can be of use to you, come and take it."

MADAME ARKADIN. I hope all your things are packed?

TRIGORIN (*impatiently*). Yes, yes. (*Musing*) Why is it that I feel so much sorrow in that appeal from a pure soul and that it wrings my heart so painfully? "If ever my life can be of use to you, come and take it." (*To* MADAME ARKADIN) Let us stay one day longer.

(MADAME ARKADIN *shakes her head.*)

TRIGORIN. Let us stay!

MADAME ARKADIN. Darling, I know what keeps you here. But have control over yourself. You are a little intoxicated, try to be sober.

TRIGORIN. You be sober too, be sensible and reasonable, I implore you; look at it all as a true friend should. (*Presses her hand*) You are capable of sacrifice. Be a friend to me, let me be free!

MADAME ARKADIN (*in violent agitation*). Are you so enthralled?

TRIGORIN. I am drawn to her! Perhaps it is just what I need.

MADAME ARKADIN. The love of a provincial girl? Oh, how little you know yourself!

TRIGORIN. Sometimes people sleep as they talk—that's how it is with me, I am talking to you and yet I am asleep and dreaming of her.... I am possessed by sweet, marvellous dreams.... Let me be free....

MADAME ARKADIN (*trembling*). No, no! I am an ordinary woman, you can't talk like that to me. Don't torture me, Boris. It terrifies me.

TRIGORIN. If you cared to, you could be not ordinary. Love—youthful, charming, poetical, lifting one into a world of dreams—that's the only thing in life that can give happiness! I have never yet known a love like that.... In my youth I never had time, I was always hanging about the editors' offices, struggling with want. Now it is here, that love, it has come, it beckons to me. What sense is there in running away from it?

MADAME ARKADIN (*wrathfully*). You have gone mad!

TRIGORIN. Well, let me?

MADAME ARKADIN. You are all in a conspiracy together to torment me to-day! (*Weeps.*)

TRIGORIN (*clutching at his heart*). She does not understand! She won't understand!

MADAME ARKADIN. Am I so old and ugly that you don't mind talking of other women to me? (*Puts her arms round him and kisses him.*) Oh, you are mad! My wonderful, splendid darling.... You are the last

page of my life! (*Falls on her knees.*) My joy, my pride, my bliss!...
(*Embraces his knees.*) If you forsake me even for one hour I shall not
survive it, I shall go mad, my marvellous, magnificent one, my master....

TRIGORIN. Someone may come in (*helps her to get up*).

MADAME ARKADIN. Let them, I am not ashamed of my love for you
(*kisses his hands*). My treasure, you desperate boy, you want to be
mad, but I won't have it, I won't let you ... (*laughs*). You are mine ...
mine.... This forehead is mine, and these eyes, and this lovely silky
hair is mine too ... you are mine all over. You are so gifted, so clever,
the best of all modern writers, you are the one hope of Russia....
You have so much truthfulness, simplicity, freshness, healthy humour.... In one touch you can give all the essential characteristics
of a person or a landscape, your characters are living. One can't
read you without delight! You think this is exaggerated? That I am
flattering you? But look into my eyes ... look.... Do I look like a
liar? You see, I am the only one who can appreciate you; I am the
only one who tells you the truth, my precious, wonderful darling.... Are you coming? Yes? You won't abandon me?...

TRIGORIN. I have no will of my own ... I have never had a will of my
own.... Flabby, feeble, always submissive—how can a woman care
for such a man? Take me, carry me off, but don't let me move a step
away from you....

MADAME ARKADIN (*to herself*). Now he is mine! (*In an easy tone as though
nothing had happened*) But, of course, if you like, you can stay. I'll go
by myself and you can come afterwards, a week later. After all, why
should you be in a hurry?

TRIGORIN. No, we may as well go together.

MADAME ARKADIN. As you please. Let us go together then (*a pause*).

(TRIGORIN *makes a note.*)

MADAME ARKADIN. What are you writing?

TRIGORIN. I heard a good name this morning, "The Maiden's Forest."
It may be of use (*stretches*). So we are to go then? Again there will be
railway carriages, stations, refreshment bars, mutton chops, conversations....

SHAMRAEV (*enters*). I have the honour to announce, with regret, that the horses are ready. It's time, honoured lady, to set off for the station; the train comes in at five minutes past two. So please do me a favour, Irina Nikolayevna, do not forget to inquire what has become of the actor Suzdaltsev. Is he alive and well? We used to drink together at one time.... In "The Plundered Mail" he used to play incomparably ... I remember the tragedian Izmaïlov, also a remarkable personality, acted with him in Elisavetograd.... Don't be in a hurry, honoured lady, you need not start for five minutes. Once they were acting conspirators in a melodrama and when they were suddenly discovered Izmaïlov had to say, "We are caught in a trap," but he said, "We are caught in a tap!" (*Laughs*) A tap!

(*While he is speaking* YAKOV *is busy looking after the luggage. The maid brings* MADAME ARKADIN *her hat, her coat, her umbrella and her gloves; they all help* MADAME ARKADIN *to put on her things. The man-cook looks in at the door on left and after some hesitation comes in. Enter* POLINA ANDREYEVNA, *then* SORIN *and* MEDVEDENKO.)

POLINA (*with a basket*). Here are some plums for the journey.... Very sweet ones. You may be glad to have something nice....

MADAME ARKADIN. You are very kind, Polina Andreyevna.

POLINA. Good-bye, my dear! If anything has not been to your liking, forgive it (*weeps*).

MADAME ARKADIN (*embraces her*). Everything has been nice, everything! But you mustn't cry.

POLINA. The time flies so fast!

MADAME ARKADIN. There's no help for it.

SORIN (*in a great-coat with a cape to it, with his hat on and a stick in his hand, enters from door on left, crossing the stage*). Sister, it's time to start, or you may be too late after all. I am going to get into the carriage (*goes out*).

MEDVEDENKO. And I shall walk to the station ... to see you off. I'll be there in no time ... (*goes out*).

MADAME ARKADIN. Good-bye, dear friends.... If we are all alive and well, we shall meet again next summer. (*The maid, the cook and* YAKOV *kiss her hand.*) Don't forget me. (*Gives the cook a rouble*) Here's a rouble for the three of you.

THE COOK. We humbly thank you, madame! Good journey to you! We are very grateful for your kindness!

YAKOV. May God give you good luck!

SHAMRAEV. You might rejoice our hearts with a letter! Good-bye, Boris Alexeyevitch!

MADAME ARKADIN. Where is Konstantin? Tell him that I am starting; I must say good-bye. Well, don't remember evil against me. (*To* YAKOV) I gave the cook a rouble. It's for the three of you.

(*All go out on right. The stage is empty. Behind the scenes the noise that is usual when people are being seen off. The maid comes back to fetch the basket of plums from the table and goes out again.*)

TRIGORIN (*coming back*). I have forgotten my stick. I believe it is out there, on the verandah (*goes and, at door on left, meets* NINA *who is coming in*). Is that you? We are going....

NINA. I felt that we should see each other once more. (*Excitedly*) Boris Alexeyevitch, I have come to a decision, the die is cast, I am going on the stage. I shall be gone from here to-morrow; I am leaving my father, I am abandoning everything, I am beginning a new life. Like you, I am going ... to Moscow. We shall meet there.

TRIGORIN (*looking round*). Stay at the "Slavyansky Bazaar" ... Let me know at once ... Molchanovka, Groholsky House.... I am in a hurry ... (*a pause*).

NINA. One minute more....

TRIGORIN (*in an undertone*). You are so lovely.... Oh, what happiness to think that we shall see each other soon! (*She sinks on his breast.*) I shall see again those wonderful eyes, that inexpressibly beautiful tender smile ... those soft features, the expression of angelic purity.... My darling ... (*a prolonged kiss*).

CURTAIN.

(*Between the Third and Fourth Acts there is an interval of two years.*)

ACT IV

One of the drawing-rooms in SORIN'S *house, which has been turned into a study
for* KONSTANTIN TREPLEV. *On the right and left, doors leading to inner apart-
ments. In the middle, glass door leading on to the verandah. Besides the usual
drawing-room furniture there is, in corner on right, a writing-table, near door
on left, a sofa, a bookcase and books in windows and on the chairs. Evening.
There is a single lamp alight with a shade on it. It is half dark. There is the
sound of the trees rustling, and the wind howling in the chimney. A watchman
is tapping. Enter* MEDVEDENKO *and* MASHA.

MASHA (*calling*). Konstantin Gavrilitch! Konstantin Gavrilitch! (*Looking
round*) No, there is no one here. The old man keeps asking every
minute, where is Kostya, where is Kostya? He cannot live without
him....

MEDVEDENKO. He is afraid of being alone. (*Listening*) What awful
weather! This is the second day of it.

MASHA (*turns up the lamp*). There are waves on the lake. Great big ones.

MEDVEDENKO. How dark it is in the garden! We ought to have told
them to break up that stage in the garden. It stands as bare and ugly
as a skeleton, and the curtain flaps in the wind. When I passed it
yesterday evening, it seemed as though someone were crying in it.

MASHA. What next ... (*a pause*).

MEDVEDENKO. Let us go home, Masha.

MASHA (*shakes her head*). I shall stay here for the night.

MEDVEDENKO (*in an imploring voice*). Masha, do come! Our baby must
be hungry.

MASHA. Nonsense. Matryona will feed him (*a pause*).

MEDVEDENKO. I am sorry for him. He has been three nights now without his mother.

MASHA. You are a bore. In old days you used at least to discuss general subjects, but now it is only home, baby, home, baby—that's all one can get out of you.

MEDVEDENKO. Come along, Masha!

MASHA. Go by yourself.

MEDVEDENKO. Your father won't let me have a horse.

MASHA. Yes, he will. You ask, and he will.

MEDVEDENKO. Very well, I'll ask. Then you will come to-morrow?

MASHA (*taking a pinch of snuff*). Very well, to-morrow. How you pester me.

(*Enter* TREPLEV *and* POLINA ANDREYEVNA; TREPLEV *brings in pillows and a quilt, and* POLINA ANDREYEVNA *sheets and pillow-cases; they lay them on the sofa, then* TREPLEV *goes to his table and sits down.*)

MASHA. What's this for, mother?

POLINA. Pyotr Nikolayevitch asked us to make a bed for him in Kostya's room.

MASHA. Let me do it (*makes the bed*).

POLINA (*sighing*). Old people are like children (*goes up to the writing-table, and leaning on her elbow, looks at the manuscript; a pause*).

MEDVEDENKO. Well, I am going then. Good-bye, Masha (*kisses his wife's hand*). Good-bye, mother (*tries to kiss his mother-in-law's hand*).

POLINA (*with vexation*). Come, if you are going, go.

MEDVEDENKO. Good-bye, Konstantin Gavrilitch.

(TREPLEV *gives him his hand without speaking;* MEDVEDENKO *goes out.*)

POLINA (*looking at the MS.*). No one would have guessed or thought that you would have become a real author, Kostya. And now, thank God, they send you money from the magazines. (*Passes her hand over his hair*) And you have grown good-looking too.... Dear, good Kostya, do be a little kinder to my Mashenka!

MASHA (*as she makes the bed*). Leave him alone, mother.

POLINA (*to* TREPLEV). She is a nice little thing (*a pause*). A woman wants nothing, you know, Kostya, so long as you give her a kind look. I know from myself.

(TREPLEV *gets up from the table and walks away without speaking.*)

MASHA. Now you have made him angry. What induced you to pester him?

POLINA. I feel so sorry for you, Mashenka.

MASHA. Much use that is!

POLINA. My heart aches for you. I see it all, you know, I understand it all.

MASHA. It's all foolishness. There is no such thing as hopeless love except in novels. It's of no consequence. The only thing is one mustn't let oneself go and keep expecting something, waiting for the tide to turn.... When love gets into the heart there is nothing to be done but to clear it out. Here they promised to transfer my husband to another district. As soon as I am there, I shall forget it all.... I shall tear it out of my heart.

(*Two rooms away a melancholy waltz is played.*)

POLINA. That's Kostya playing. He must be depressed.

MASHA (*noiselessly dances a few waltz steps*). The great thing, mother, is not to have him before one's eyes. If they only give my Semyon his transfer, trust me, I shall get over it in a month. It's all nonsense.

(*Door on left opens.* DORN *and* MEDVEDENKO *wheel in* SORIN *in his chair.*)

MEDVEDENKO. I have six of them at home now. And flour is two kopeks per pound.

DORN. You've got to look sharp to make both ends meet.

MEDVEDENKO. It's all very well for you to laugh. You've got more money than you know what to do with.

DORN. Money? After thirty years of practice, my boy, troublesome work during which I could not call my soul my own by day or by night, I only succeeded in saving two thousand roubles, and that I spent not long ago abroad. I have nothing.

MASHA (*to her husband*). You have not gone?

MEDVEDENKO (*guiltily*). Well, how can I when they won't let me have a horse?

MASHA (*with bitter vexation in an undertone*). I can't bear the sight of you.

(*The wheel-chair remains in the left half of the room;* POLINA ANDREYEVNA, MASHA *and* DORN *sit down beside it,* MEDVEDENKO *moves mournfully to one side.*)

DORN. What changes there have been here! The drawing-room has been turned into a study.

MASHA. It is more convenient for Konstantin Gavrilitch to work here. Whenever he likes, he can walk out into the garden and think there.

(*A watchman taps.*)

SORIN. Where is my sister?

DORN. She has gone to the station to meet Trigorin. She will be back directly.

SORIN. Since you thought it necessary to send for my sister, I must be dangerously ill. (*After a silence*) It's a queer thing, I am dangerously ill and here they don't give me any medicines.

DORN. Well, what would you like to have? Valerian drops? Soda? Quinine?

SORIN. Ah, he is at his moralising again! What an infliction it is! (*With a motion of his head towards the sofa*) Is that bed for me?

POLINA. Yes, it's for you, Pyotr Nikolayevitch.

SORIN. Thank you.

DORN (*hums*). "The moon is floating in the midnight sky."

SORIN. I want to give Kostya a subject for a story. It ought to be called "The Man who Wished"—*L'homme qui a voulu.* In my youth I wanted to become a literary man—and didn't; I wanted to speak well—and I spoke horribly badly, (*mimicking himself*) "and all the rest of it, and all that, and so on, and so forth" … and I would go plodding on and on, trying to sum up till I was in a regular perspiration; I wanted to get married—and I didn't; I always wanted to live in town and here I am ending my life in the country—and so on.

DORN. I wanted to become an actual civil councillor—and I have.

SORIN (*laughs*). That I had no hankerings after. That happened of itself.

DORN. To be expressing dissatisfaction with life at sixty-two is really ungracious, you know.

SORIN. What a persistent fellow he is! You might understand that one wants to live!

DORN. That's just frivolity. It's the law of nature that every life must have an end.

SORIN. You argue like a man who has had enough. You are satisfied and so you are indifferent to life, nothing matters to you. But even you will be afraid to die.

DORN. The dread of death is an animal fear. One must overcome it. A rational fear of death is only possible for those who believe in eternal life and are conscious of their sins. And you, in the first place, don't believe, and, in the second, what sins have you to worry about? You have served in the courts of justice for twenty-five years—that's all.

SORIN (*laughs*). Twenty-eight....

(TREPLEV *comes in and sits down on a stool at* SORIN'S *feet.* MASHA *never takes her eyes off him.*)

DORN. We are hindering Konstantin Gavrilitch from working.

TREPLEV. Oh no, it doesn't matter (*a pause*).

MEDVEDENKO. Allow me to ask you, doctor, what town did you like best abroad?

DORN. Genoa.

TREPLEV. Why Genoa?

DORN. The life in the streets is so wonderful there. When you go out of the hotel in the evening, the whole street is packed with people. You wander aimlessly zigzagging about among the crowd, backwards and forwards; you live with it, are psychologically at one with it and begin almost to believe that a world-soul is really possible, such as was acted by Nina Zaretchny in your play. And, by the way, where is she now? How is she getting on?

TREPLEV. I expect she is quite well.

DORN. I was told that she was leading a rather peculiar life. How was that?

TREPLEV. That's a long story, doctor.

DORN. Well, tell it us shortly (*a pause*).

TREPLEV. She ran away from home and had an affair with Trigorin. You know that?

DORN. I know.

TREPLEV. She had a child. The child died. Trigorin got tired of her and went back to his old ties, as might have been expected. Though, indeed, he had never abandoned them, but in his weak-willed way contrived to keep both going. As far as I can make out from what I have heard, Nina's private life was a complete failure.

DORN. And the stage?

TREPLEV. I fancy that was worse still. She made her début at some holiday place near Moscow, then went to the provinces. All that time I did not lose sight of her, and wherever she went I followed her. She always took big parts, but she acted crudely, without taste, screamingly, with violent gestures. There were moments when she uttered a cry successfully or died successfully, but they were only moments.

DORN. Then she really has some talent?

TREPLEV. It was difficult to make it out. I suppose she has. I saw her but she would not see me, and the servants would not admit me at the hotel. I understood her state of mind and did not insist on seeing her (*a pause*). What more can I tell you? Afterwards, when I was back at home, I had some letters from her—warm, intelligent, interesting letters. She did not complain, but I felt that she was profoundly unhappy; every line betrayed sick overstrained nerves. And her imagination is a little unhinged. She signed herself the Sea-gull. In Pushkin's "Mermaid" the miller says that he is a raven, and in the same way in her letters she kept repeating that she was a sea-gull. Now she is here.

DORN. Here? How do you mean?

TREPLEV. In the town, staying at an inn. She has been there for five days. I did go to see her, and Marya Ilyinishna here went too, but she won't see anyone. Semyon Semyonitch declares he saw her yesterday afternoon in the fields a mile and a half from here.

MEDVEDENKO. Yes, I saw her. She went in that direction, towards the town. I bowed to her and asked her why she did not come to see us. She said she would come.

TREPLEV. She won't come (*a pause*). Her father and stepmother refuse to recognise her. They have put watchmen about so that she may not even go near the house (*walks away with the doctor towards the writing table*). How easy it is to be a philosopher on paper, doctor, and how difficult it is in life!

SORIN. She was a charming girl.

DORN. What?

SORIN. She was a charming girl, I say. Actual Civil Councillor Sorin was positively in love with her for a time.

DORN. The old Lovelace.

(*SHAMRAEV's laugh is heard.*)

POLINA. I fancy our people have come back from the station....

TREPLEV. Yes, I hear Mother.

(*Enter* MADAME ARKADIN, TRIGORIN *and with them* SHAMRAEV.)

SHAMRAEV (*as he enters*). We all grow old and dilapidated under the influence of the elements, while you, honoured lady, are still young ... a light blouse, sprightliness, grace....

MADAME ARKADIN. You want to bring me ill-luck again, you tiresome man!

TRIGORIN. How do you do, Pyotr Nikolayevitch! So you are still poorly? That's bad! (*Seeing* MASHA, *joyfully*) Marya Ilyinishna!

MASHA. You know me, do you? (*shakes hands*).

TRIGORIN. Married?

MASHA. Long ago.

TRIGORIN. Are you happy? (*Bows to* DORN *and* MEDVEDENKO, *then hesitatingly approaches* TREPLEV) Irina Nikolayevna has told me that you have forgotten the past and are no longer angry.

(*TREPLEV holds out his hand.*)

MADAME ARKADIN (*to her son*). Boris Alexeyevitch has brought the magazine with your new story in it.

TREPLEV (*taking the magazine, to* TRIGORIN). Thank you, you are very kind. (*They sit down.*)

TRIGORIN. Your admirers send their greetings to you.... In Petersburg and Moscow there is great interest in your work and I am continually being asked questions about you. People ask what you are like, how old you are, whether you are dark or fair. Everyone imagines, for some reason, that you are no longer young. And no one knows your real name, as you always publish under a pseudonym. You are as mysterious as the Iron Mask.

TREPLEV. Will you be able to make a long stay?

TRIGORIN. No, I think I must go back to Moscow to-morrow. I am obliged to. I am in a hurry to finish my novel, and besides, I have promised something for a collection of tales that is being published. It's the old story, in fact.

(*While they are talking* MADAME ARKADIN *and* POLINA ANDREYEVNA *put a card-table in the middle of the room and open it out.* SHAMRAEV *lights candles and sets chairs. A game of loto is brought out of the cupboard.*)

TRIGORIN. The weather has not given me a friendly welcome. There is a cruel wind. If it has dropped by to-morrow morning I shall go to the lake to fish. And I must have a look at the garden and that place where—you remember?—your play was acted. I've got a subject for a story, I only want to revive my recollections of the scene in which it is laid.

MASHA (*to her father*). Father, let my husband have a horse! He must get home.

SHAMRAEV (*mimicking*). Must get home—a horse! (*Sternly*) You can see for yourself: they have just been to the station. I can't send them out again.

MASHA. But there are other horses. (*Seeing that her father says nothing, waves her hand*) There's no doing anything with you.

MEDVEDENKO. I can walk, Masha. Really....

POLINA (*with a sigh*). Walk in such weather ... (*sits down to the card-table*). Come, friends.

MEDVEDENKO. It is only four miles. Good-bye (*kisses his wife's hand*). Good-bye, mother. (*His mother-in-law reluctantly holds out her hand for him to kiss.*) I wouldn't trouble anyone, but the baby ... (*bows to the company*). Good-bye ... (*goes out with a guilty step*).

SHAMRAEV. He can walk right enough. He's not a general.

POLINA (*tapping on the table*). Come, friends. Don't let us waste time, we shall soon be called to supper.

(SHAMRAEV, MASHA *and* DORN *sit down at the table.*)

MADAME ARKADIN (*to* TRIGORIN). When the long autumn evenings come on, they play loto here. Look, it's the same old loto that we had when our mother used to play with us, when we were children. Won't you have a game before supper? (*Sits down to the table with* TRIGORIN.) It's a dull game, but it is not so bad when you are used to it (*deals three cards to everyone*).

TREPLEV (*turning the pages of the magazine*). He has read his own story, but he has not even cut mine (*puts the magazine down on the writing-table, then goes towards door on left; as he passes his mother he kisses her on the head*).

MADAME ARKADIN. And you, Kostya?

TREPLEV. Excuse me, I would rather not ... I am going out (*goes out*).

MADAME ARKADIN. The stake is ten kopeks. Put it down for me, doctor, will you?

DORN. Right.

MASHA. Has everyone put down their stakes? I begin ... Twenty-two.

MADAME ARKADIN. Yes.

MASHA. Three!

DORN. Right!

MASHA. Did you play three? Eight! Eighty-one! Ten!

SHAMRAEV. Don't be in a hurry!

MADAME ARKADIN. What a reception I had in Harkov! My goodness! I feel dizzy with it still.

MASHA. Thirty-four!

(*A melancholy waltz is played behind the scenes.*)

MADAME ARKADIN. The students gave me an ovation.... Three baskets of flowers ... two wreaths and this, see (*unfastens a brooch on her throat and lays it on the table*).

SHAMRAEV. Yes, that is a thing....

MASHA. Fifty!

DORN. Exactly fifty?

MADAME ARKADIN. I had a wonderful dress.... Whatever I don't know, I do know how to dress.

POLINA. Kostya is playing the piano; he is depressed, poor fellow.

SHAMRAEV. He is awfully abused in the newspapers.

MASHA. Seventy-seven!

MADAME ARKADIN. As though that mattered!

TRIGORIN. He never quite comes off. He has not yet hit upon his own medium. There is always something queer and vague, at times almost like delirium. Not a single living character.

MASHA. Eleven!

MADAME ARKADIN (*looking round at* SORIN). Petrusha, are you bored? (*A pause.*) He is asleep.

DORN. The actual civil councillor is asleep.

MASHA. Seven! Ninety!

TRIGORIN. If I lived in such a place, beside a lake, do you suppose I should write? I should overcome this passion and should do nothing but fish.

MASHA. Twenty-eight!

TRIGORIN. Catching perch is so delightful!

DORN. Well, I believe in Konstantin Gavrilitch. There is something in him! There is something in him! He thinks in images; his stories are vivid, full of colour and they affect me strongly. The only pity is that he has not got definite aims. He produces an impression and that's all, but you can't get far with nothing but an impression. Irina Nikolayevna, are you glad that your son is a writer?

MADAME ARKADIN. Only fancy, I have not read anything of his yet. I never have time.

MASHA. Twenty-six!

(TREPLEV *comes in quietly and sits down at his table.*)

SHAMRAEV (*to* TRIGORIN). We have still got something here belonging to you, Boris Alexeyevitch.

TRIGORIN. What's that?

SHAMRAEV. Konstantin Gavrilitch shot a sea-gull and you asked me to get it stuffed for you.

TRIGORIN. I don't remember! (*Pondering*) I don't remember!

MASHA. Sixty-six! One!

TREPLEV (*flinging open the window, listens*). How dark it is! I don't know why I feel so uneasy.

MADAME ARKADIN. Kostya, shut the window, there's a draught.

(TREPLEV *shuts the window.*)

MASHA. Eighty-eight!

TRIGORIN. The game is mine!

MADAME ARKADIN (*gaily*). Bravo, bravo!

SHAMRAEV. Bravo!

MADAME ARKADIN. That man always has luck in everything (*gets up*). And now let us go and have something to eat. Our great man has not dined to-day. We will go on again after supper. (*To her son*) Kostya, leave your manuscripts and come to supper.

TREPLEV. I don't want any, Mother, I am not hungry.

MADAME ARKADIN. As you like. (*Wakes* SORIN) Petrusha, supper! (*Takes* SHAMRAEV'S *arm*) I'll tell you about my reception in Harkov.

(POLINA ANDREYEVNA *puts out the candles on the table. Then she and* DORN *wheel the chair. All go out by door on left; only* TREPLEV, *sitting at the writing-table, is left on the stage.*)

TREPLEV (*settling himself to write; runs through what he has written already*). I have talked so much about new forms and now I feel that little by little I am falling into a convention myself. (*Reads*) "The placard on the wall proclaimed.... The pale face in its setting of dark hair." Proclaimed, setting. That's stupid (*scratches out*). I will begin where the hero is awakened by the patter of the rain, and throw out all the rest. The description of the moonlight evening is long and over-elaborate. Trigorin has worked out methods for himself, it's easy for him now.... With him the broken bottle neck glitters on the dam and the mill-wheel casts a black shadow—and there you have the moonlight night, while I have the tremulous light, and the soft twinkling of the stars, and the far-away strains of the piano dying away in the still fragrant air.... It's agonising (*a pause*). I come more and more to the conviction that it is not a question of new and old forms, but that what matters is that a man should write without thinking about forms at all, write because it springs freely from his soul. (*There is a tap at the window nearest to the table*) What is that? (*Looks out of window*) There is nothing to be seen ... (*opens the glass door and looks out into the garden*). Someone ran down the steps. (*Calls*) Who is there? (*Goes out and can be heard walking rapidly along the verandah; returns half a minute later with* NINA ZARETCHNY.) Nina, Nina!

(NINA *lays her head on his breast and weeps with subdued sobs.*)

TREPLEV (*moved*). Nina! Nina! It's you ... you.... It's as though I had foreseen it, all day long my heart has been aching and restless (*takes off her hat and cape*). Oh, my sweet, my precious, she has come at last. Don't let us cry, don't let us!

NINA. There is someone here.

TREPLEV. No one.

NINA. Lock the doors, someone may come in.

TREPLEV. No one will come in.

NINA. I know Irina Nikolayevna is here. Lock the doors.

TREPLEV (*locks the door on right, goes to door on left*). There is no lock on this one. I'll put a chair against it (*puts an armchair against the door*). Don't be afraid, no one will come.

NINA (*looking intently into his face*). Let me look at you. (*Looking round*) It's warm, it's nice.... In old days this was the drawing-room. Am I very much changed?

TREPLEV. Yes ... You are thinner and your eyes are bigger. Nina, how strange it is that I should be seeing you. Why would not you let me see you? Why haven't you come all this time? I know you have been here almost a week.... I have been to you several times every day; I stood under your window like a beggar.

NINA. I was afraid that you might hate me. I dream every night that you look at me and don't know me. If only you knew! Ever since I came I have been walking here ... by the lake. I have been near your house many times and could not bring myself to enter it. Let us sit down. (*They sit down.*) Let us sit down and talk and talk. It's nice here, it's warm and snug. Do you hear the wind? There's a passage in Turgenev, "Well for the man on such a night who sits under the shelter of home, who has a warm corner in safety." I am a sea-gull.... No, that's not it (*rubs her forehead*). What was I saying? Yes ... Turgenev ... "And the Lord help all homeless wanderers!" ... It doesn't matter (*sobs*).

TREPLEV. Nina, you are crying again.... Nina!

NINA. Never mind, it does me good ... I haven't cried for two years. Yesterday, late in the evening, I came into the garden to see whether our stage was still there. It is still standing. I cried for the first time after two years and it eased the weight on my heart and made it lighter. You see, I am not crying now (*takes him by the hand*). And so now you are an author.... You are an author, I am an actress.... We too have been drawn into the whirlpool. I lived joyously like a child—I woke up singing in the morning; I loved you and dreamed of fame, and now? Early to-morrow morning I must go to Yelets third-class ... with peasants, and at Yelets the cultured tradesmen will pester me with attentions. Life is a coarse business!

TREPLEV. Why to Yelets?

NINA. I have taken an engagement for the whole winter. It is time to go.

TREPLEV. Nina, I cursed you, I hated you, I tore up your letters and photographs, but I was conscious every minute that my soul is bound to yours for ever. It's not in my power to leave off loving you, Nina. Ever since I lost you and began to get my work published my life has been unbearable—I am wretched.... My youth was, as it were, torn away all at once and it seems to me as though I have lived for ninety years already. I call upon you, I kiss the earth on which you have walked; wherever I look I see your face, that tender smile that lighted up the best days of my life....

NINA (*distractedly*). Why does he talk like this, why does he talk like this?

TREPLEV. I am alone in the world, warmed by no affection. I am as cold as though I were in a cellar, and everything I write is dry, hard and gloomy. Stay here, Nina, I entreat you, or let me go with you!

(NINA *rapidly puts on her hat and cape.*)

TREPLEV. Nina, why is this? For God's sake, Nina! (*Looks at her as she puts her things on; a pause.*)

NINA. My horses are waiting at the gate. Don't see me off, I'll go alone.... (*Through her tears*) Give me some water....

TREPLEV (*gives her some water*). Where are you going now?

NINA. To the town (*a pause*). Is Irina Nikolayevna here?

TREPLEV. Yes.... Uncle was taken worse on Thursday and we telegraphed for her.

NINA. Why do you say that you kissed the earth on which I walked? I ought to be killed. (*Bends over table*) I am so tired! If I could rest ... if I could rest! (*Raising her head*) I am a sea-gull.... No, that's not it. I am an actress. Oh, well! (*Hearing* MADAME ARKADIN *and* TRIGORIN *laughing, she listens, then runs to door on left and looks through the keyhole.*) He is here too.... (*Turning back to* TREPLEV) Oh, well ... it doesn't matter ... no.... He did not believe in the stage, he always laughed at my dreams and little by little I left off believing in it too, and lost heart.... And then I was fretted by love and jealousy, and continually anxious over my little one.... I grew petty and trivial, I acted stupidly.... I did not know what to do with my arms, I did not know how to stand on the stage, could not control my voice. You can't understand what it feels like when one knows one is acting disgracefully. I am a sea-gull. No, that's not it.... Do you remember you shot a sea-gull? A man came by chance, saw it and, just to pass the time, destroyed it.... A subject for a short story.... That's not it, though (*rubs her forehead*). What was I saying? ... I am talking of the stage. Now I am not like that. I am a real actress, I act with enjoyment, with enthusiasm, I am intoxicated when I am on the stage and feel that I am splendid. And since I have been here, I keep walking about and thinking, thinking and feeling that my soul is getting stronger every day. Now I know, I understand, Kostya, that in our work—in acting or writing—what matters is not fame, not glory, not what I dreamed of, but knowing how to be patient. To bear one's cross and have faith. I have faith and it all doesn't hurt so much, and when I think of my vocation I am not afraid of life.

TREPLEV (*mournfully*). You have found your path, you know which way you are going, but I am still floating in a chaos of dreams and images, not knowing what use it is to anyone. I have no faith and don't know what my vocation is.

NINA (*listening*). 'Sh-sh ... I am going. Good-bye. When I become a great actress, come and look at me. Will you promise? But now ... (*presses his hand*) it's late. I can hardly stand on my feet.... I am worn out and hungry....

TREPLEV. Stay, I'll give you some supper.

NINA. No, no.... Don't see me off, I will go by myself. My horses are close by.... So she brought him with her? Well, it doesn't matter. When you see Trigorin, don't say anything to him.... I love him! I love him even more than before.... A subject for a short story ... I love him, I love him passionately, I love him to despair. It was nice in old days, Kostya! Do you remember? How clear, warm, joyous and pure life was, what feelings we had—feelings like tender, exquisite flowers.... Do you remember? (*Recites*) "Men, lions, eagles, and partridges, horned deer, geese, spiders, silent fish that dwell in the water, star-fishes, and creatures which cannot be seen by the eye—all living things, all living things, all living things, have completed their cycle of sorrow, are extinct.... For thousands of years the earth has borne no living creature on its surface, and this poor moon lights its lamp in vain. On the meadow the cranes no longer waken with a cry and there is no sound of the May beetles in the lime trees ..." (*impulsively embraces* TREPLEV *and runs out of the glass door*).

TREPLEV (*after a pause*). It will be a pity if someone meets her in the garden and tells mother. It may upset Mother....

(*He spends two minutes in tearing up all his manuscripts and throwing them under the table; then unlocks the door on right and goes out.*)

DORN (*trying to open the door on left*). Strange. The door seems to be locked ... (*comes in and puts the armchair in its place*). An obstacle race.

(*Enter* MADAME ARKADIN *and* POLINA ANDREYEVNA, *behind them* YAKOV *carrying a tray with bottles;* MASHA; *then* SHAMRAEV *and* TRIGORIN.)

MADAME ARKADIN. Put the claret and the beer for Boris Alexeyevitch here on the table. We will play as we drink it. Let us sit down, friends.

POLINA (*to* YAKOV). Bring tea too at the same time (*lights the candles and sits down to the card-table*).

SHAMRAEV (*leads* TRIGORIN *to the cupboard*). Here's the thing I was speaking about just now (*takes the stuffed sea-gull from the cupboard*). This is what you ordered.

TRIGORIN (*looking at the sea-gull*). I don't remember it. (*Musing*) I don't remember.

(*The sound of a shot coming from right of stage; everyone starts.*)

MADAME ARKADIN (*frightened*). What's that?

DORN. That's nothing. It must be something in my medicine-chest that has gone off. Don't be anxious (*goes out at door on right, comes back in half a minute*). That's what it is. A bottle of ether has exploded. (*Hums*) "I stand before thee enchanted again...."

MADAME ARKADIN (*sitting down to the table*). Ough, how frightened I was. It reminded me of how ... (*hides her face in her hands*). It made me quite dizzy....

DORN (*turning over the leaves of the magazine, to* TRIGORIN). There was an article in this two months ago—a letter from America—and I wanted to ask you, among other things (*puts his arm round* TRIGORIN'S *waist and leads him to the footlights*) as I am very much interested in the question.... (*In a lower tone, dropping his voice*) Get Irina Nikolayevna away somehow. The fact is, Konstantin Gavrilitch has shot himself....

CURTAIN.

THREE SISTERS

First performed in Moscow,

January 1901

CHARACTERS IN THE PLAY

ANDREY SERGEYEVITCH PROZOROV.

NATALYA IVANOVNA, *also called* NATASHA (*his fiancée, afterwards his wife*).

OLGA
MASHA } (*his sisters*).
IRINA

FYODOR ILYITCH KULIGIN (*a high-school teacher, husband of* MASHA).

LIEUTENANT-COLONEL ALEXANDR IGNATYEVITCH VERSHININ (*battery-commander*).

BARON NIKOLAY LVOVITCH TUSENBACH (*lieutenant*).

VASSILY VASSILYEVITCH SOLYONY (*captain*).

IVAN ROMANITCH TCHEBUTYKIN (*army doctor*).

ALEXEY PETROVITCH FEDOTIK (*second lieutenant*).

VLADIMIR KARLOVITCH RODDEY (*second lieutenant*).

FERAPONT (*an old porter from the Rural Board*).

ANFISA (*the nurse, an old woman of eighty*).

The action takes place in a provincial town.

ACT I

In the house of the PROZOROVS. *A drawing-room with columns beyond which a large room is visible. Mid-day; it is bright and sunny. The table in the farther room is being laid for lunch.*

OLGA, *in the dark blue uniform of a high-school teacher, is correcting exercise books, at times standing still and then walking up and down;* MASHA, *in a black dress, with her hat on her knee, is reading a book;* IRINA, *in a white dress, is standing plunged in thought.*

OLGA. Father died just a year ago, on this very day—the fifth of May, your name-day, Irina. It was very cold, snow was falling. I felt as though I should not live through it; you lay fainting as though you were dead. But now a year has passed and we can think of it calmly; you are already in a white dress, your face is radiant. (*The clock strikes twelve.*) The clock was striking then too (*a pause*). I remember the band playing and the firing at the cemetery as they carried the coffin. Though he was a general in command of a brigade, yet there weren't many people there. It was raining, though. Heavy rain and snow.

IRINA. Why recall it!

(BARON TUSENBACH, TCHEBUTYKIN *and* SOLYONY *appear near the table in the dining-room, beyond the columns.*)

OLGA. It is warm to-day, we can have the windows open, but the birches are not in leaf yet. Father was given his brigade and came here with us from Moscow eleven years ago and I remember distinctly that in Moscow at this time, at the beginning of May, everything was already in flower; it was warm, and everything was bathed in sunshine. It's eleven years ago, and yet I remember it all as though we had left it yesterday. Oh, dear! I woke up this morning, I saw a blaze of sunshine. I saw the spring, and joy stirred in my heart. I had a passionate longing to be back at home again!

TCHEBUTYKIN. The devil it is!

TUSENBACH. Of course, it's nonsense.

(MASHA, *brooding over a book, softly whistles a song.*)

OLGA. Don't whistle, Masha. How can you! (*A pause.*) Being all day in school and then at my lessons till the evening gives me a perpetual headache and thoughts as gloomy as though I were old. And really these four years that I have been at the high-school I have felt my strength and my youth oozing away from me every day. And only one yearning grows stronger and stronger....

IRINA. To go back to Moscow. To sell the house, to make an end of everything here, and off to Moscow....

OLGA. Yes! To Moscow, and quickly.

(TCHEBUTYKIN *and* TUSENBACH *laugh.*)

IRINA. Andrey will probably be a professor, he will not live here anyhow. The only difficulty is poor Masha.

OLGA. Masha will come and spend the whole summer in Moscow every year.

(MASHA *softly whistles a tune.*)

IRINA. Please God it will all be managed. (*Looking out of window*) How fine it is to-day. I don't know why I feel so light-hearted! I remembered this morning that it was my name-day and at once I felt joyful and thought of my childhood when mother was living. And I was thrilled by such wonderful thoughts, such thoughts!

OLGA. You are radiant to-day and looking lovelier than usual. And Masha is lovely too. Andrey would be nice-looking, but he has grown too fat and that does not suit him. And I have grown older and ever so much thinner. I suppose it's because I get so cross with the girls at school. To-day now I am free, I am at home, and my head doesn't ache, and I feel younger than yesterday. I am only twenty-eight.... It's all quite right, it's all from God, but it seems to me that if I were married and sitting at home all day, it would be better (*a pause*). I should be fond of my husband.

TUSENBACH (*to* SOLYONY). You talk such nonsense, I am tired of listening to you. (*Coming into the drawing-room*) I forgot to tell you, you will receive a visit to-day from Vershinin, the new commander of our battery (*sits down to the piano*).

OLGA. Well, I shall be delighted.

IRINA. Is he old?

TUSENBACH. No, nothing to speak of. Forty or forty-five at the most (*softly plays the piano*). He seems to be a nice fellow. He is not stupid, that's certain. Only he talks a lot.

IRINA. Is he interesting?

TUSENBACH. Yes, he is all right, only he has a wife, a mother-in-law and two little girls. And it's his second wife too. He is paying calls and telling everyone that he has a wife and two little girls. He'll tell you so too. His wife seems a bit crazy, with her hair in a long plait like a girl's, always talks in a high-flown style, makes philosophical reflections and frequently attempts to commit suicide, evidently to annoy her husband. I should have left a woman like that years ago, but he puts up with her and merely complains.

SOLYONY (*coming into the drawing-room with* TCHEBUTYKIN). With one hand I can only lift up half a hundredweight, but with both hands I can lift up a hundredweight and a half or even a hundredweight and three-quarters. From that I conclude that two men are not only twice but three times as strong as one man, or even more....

TCHEBUTYKIN (*reading the newspaper as he comes in*). For hair falling out ... two ounces of naphthaline in half a bottle of spirit ... to be dissolved and used daily ... (*puts it down in his note-book*). Let's make a note of it! No, I don't want it ... (*scratches it out*). It doesn't matter.

IRINA. Ivan Romanitch, dear Ivan Romanitch!

TCHEBUTYKIN. What is it, my child, my joy?

IRINA. Tell me, why is it I am so happy to-day? As though I were sailing with the great blue sky above me and big white birds flying over it. Why is it? Why?

TCHEBUTYKIN (*kissing both her hands, tenderly*). My white bird....

IRINA. When I woke up this morning, got up and washed, it suddenly seemed to me as though everything in the world was clear to me and that I knew how one ought to live. Dear Ivan Romanitch, I know all about it. A man ought to work, to toil in the sweat of his brow, whoever he may be, and all the purpose and meaning of his life, his happiness, his ecstasies lie in that alone. How delightful to be a workman who gets up before dawn and breaks stones on the road, or a shepherd, or a schoolmaster teaching children, or an engine-driver.... Oh, dear! to say nothing of human beings, it would be better to be an ox, better to be a humble horse and work, than a young woman who wakes at twelve o'clock, then has coffee in bed, then spends two hours dressing.... Oh, how awful that is! Just as one has a craving for water in hot weather I have a craving for work. And if I don't get up early and work, give me up as a friend, Ivan Romanitch.

TCHEBUTYKIN (*tenderly*). I'll give you up, I'll give you up....

OLGA. Father trained us to get up at seven o'clock. Now Irina wakes at seven and lies in bed at least till nine thinking. And she looks so serious! (*Laughs.*)

IRINA. You are used to thinking of me as a child and are surprised when I look serious. I am twenty!

TUSENBACH. The yearning for work, oh dear, how well I understand it! I have never worked in my life. I was born in cold, idle Petersburg, in a family that had known nothing of work or cares of any kind. I remember, when I came home from the school of cadets, a footman used to pull off my boots. I used to be troublesome, but my mother looked at me with reverential awe, and was surprised when other people did not do the same. I was guarded from work. But I doubt if they have succeeded in guarding me completely, I doubt it! The time is at hand, an avalanche is moving down upon us, a mighty clearing storm which is coming, is already near and will soon blow the laziness, the indifference, the distaste for work, the rotten boredom out of our society. I shall work, and in another twenty-five or thirty years every one will have to work. Every one!

TCHEBUTYKIN. I am not going to work.

TUSENBACH. You don't count.

SOLYONY. In another twenty-five years you won't be here, thank God.

In two or three years you will kick the bucket, or I shall lose my temper and put a bullet through your head, my angel. (*Pulls a scent-bottle out of his pocket and sprinkles his chest and hands.*)

TCHEBUTYKIN (*laughs*). And I really have never done anything at all. I haven't done a stroke of work since I left the University, I have never read a book, I read nothing but newspapers ... (*takes another newspaper out of his pocket*). Here ... I know, for instance, from the newspapers that there was such a person as Dobrolyubov, but what he wrote, I can't say.... Goodness only knows.... (*A knock is heard on the floor from the storey below.*) There ... they are calling me downstairs, someone has come for me. I'll be back directly.... Wait a minute ... (*goes out hurriedly, combing his beard*).

IRINA. He's got something up his sleeve.

TUSENBACH. Yes, he went out with a solemn face, evidently he is just going to bring you a present.

IRINA. What a nuisance!

OLGA. Yes, it's awful. He is always doing something silly.

MASHA. By the sea-strand an oak-tree green ... upon that oak a chain of gold ... upon that oak a chain of gold (*gets up, humming softly*).

OLGA. You are not very cheerful to-day, Masha.

(MASHA, *humming, puts on her hat.*)

OLGA. Where are you going?

MASHA. Home.

IRINA. How queer!...

TUSENBACH. To go away from a name-day party!

MASHA. Never mind.... I'll come in the evening. Good-bye, my darling ... (*kisses* IRINA). Once again I wish you, be well and happy. In old days, when father was alive, we always had thirty or forty officers here on name-days; it was noisy, but to-day there is only a man and a half, and it is as still as the desert.... I'll go.... I am in the blues to-day, I am feeling glum, so don't you mind what I say (*laughing through her tears*). We'll talk some other time, and so for now good-bye, darling, I am going....

IRINA (*discontentedly*). Oh, how tiresome you are....

OLGA (*with tears*). I understand you, Masha.

SOLYONY. If a man philosophises, there will be philosophy or sophistry, anyway, but if a woman philosophises, or two do it, then you may just snap your fingers!

MASHA. What do you mean to say by that, you terrible person?

SOLYONY. Nothing. He had not time to say "alack," before the bear was on his back (*a pause*).

MASHA (*to* OLGA, *angrily*). Don't blubber!

(*Enter* ANFISA *and* FERAPONT *carrying a cake.*)

ANFISA. This way, my good man. Come in, your boots are clean. (*To* IRINA) From the Rural Board, from Mihail Ivanitch Protopopov.... A cake.

IRINA. Thanks. Thank him (*takes the cake*).

FERAPONT. What?

IRINA (*more loudly*). Thank him from me!

OLGA. Nurse dear, give him some pie. Ferapont, go along, they will give you some pie.

FERAPONT. Eh?

ANFISA. Come along, Ferapont Spiridonitch, my good soul, come along ... (*goes out with* FERAPONT).

MASHA. I don't like that Protopopov, that Mihail Potapitch or Ivanitch. He ought not to be invited.

IRINA. I did not invite him.

MASHA. That's a good thing.

(*Enter* TCHEBUTYKIN, *followed by an orderly with a silver samovar; a hum of surprise and displeasure.*)

OLGA (*putting her hands over her face*). A samovar! How awful! (*Goes out to the table in the dining-room.*)

IRINA. My dear Ivan Romanitch, what are you thinking about!

TUSENBACH (*laughs*). I warned you!

MASHA. Ivan Romanitch, you really have no conscience!

TCHEBUTYKIN. My dear girls, my darlings, you are all that I have, you are the most precious treasures I have on earth. I shall soon be sixty,

I am an old man, alone in the world, a useless old man.... There is nothing good in me, except my love for you, and if it were not for you, I should have been dead long ago.... (*To* IRINA) My dear, my little girl, I've known you from a baby ... I've carried you in my arms.... I loved your dear mother....

IRINA. But why such expensive presents?

TCHEBUTYKIN (*angry and tearful*). Expensive presents.... Get along with you! (*To the orderly*) Take the samovar in there ... (*Mimicking*) Expensive presents ... (*The orderly carries the samovar into the dining-room.*)

ANFISA (*crossing the room*). My dears, a colonel is here, a stranger.... He has taken off his greatcoat, children, he is coming in here. Irinushka, you must be nice and polite, dear ... (*As she goes out*) And it's time for lunch already ... mercy on us....

TUSENBACH. Vershinin, I suppose.

(*Enter* VERSHININ.)

TUSENBACH. Colonel Vershinin.

VERSHININ (*to* MASHA *and* IRINA). I have the honour to introduce myself, my name is Vershinin. I am very, very glad to be in your house at last. How you have grown up! Aie-aie!

IRINA. Please sit down. We are delighted to see you.

VERSHININ (*with animation*). How glad I am, how glad I am! But there are three of you sisters. I remember—three little girls. I don't remember your faces, but that your father, Colonel Prozorov, had three little girls I remember perfectly, and saw them with my own eyes. How time passes! Hey-ho, how it passes!

TUSENBACH. Alexandr Ignatyevitch has come from Moscow.

IRINA. From Moscow? You have come from Moscow?

VERSHININ. Yes. Your father was in command of a battery there, and I was an officer in the same brigade. (*To* MASHA) Your face, now, I seem to remember.

MASHA. I don't remember you.

IRINA. Olya! Olya! (*Calls into the dining-room*) Olya, come!

(OLGA *comes out of the dining-room into the drawing-room.*)

IRINA. Colonel Vershinin is from Moscow, it appears.

VERSHININ. So you are Olga Sergeyevna, the eldest.... And you are Marya.... And you are Irina, the youngest....

OLGA. You come from Moscow?

VERSHININ. Yes. I studied in Moscow. I began my service there, I served there for years, and at last I have been given a battery here— I have come here as you see. I don't remember you exactly, I only remember you were three sisters. I remember your father. If I shut my eyes, I can see him as though he were living. I used to visit you in Moscow....

OLGA. I thought I remembered everyone, and now all at once ...

VERSHININ. My name is Alexandr Ignatyevitch.

IRINA. Alexandr Ignatyevitch, you have come from Moscow.... What a surprise!

OLGA. We are going to move there, you know.

IRINA. We are hoping to be there by the autumn. It's our native town, we were born there.... In Old Basmanny Street ... (*both laugh with delight*).

MASHA. To see some one from our own town unexpectedly! (*Eagerly*) Now I remember! Do you remember, Olya, they used to talk of the "love-sick major"? You were a lieutenant at that time and were in love, and for some reason everyone called you "major" to tease you....

VERSHININ (*laughs*). Yes, yes.... The love-sick major, that was it.

MASHA. You only had a moustache then.... Oh, how much older you look! (*through tears*) how much older!

VERSHININ. Yes, when I was called the love-sick major I was young, I was in love. Now it's very different.

OLGA. But you haven't a single grey hair. You have grown older but you are not old.

VERSHININ. I am in my forty-third year, though. Is it long since you left Moscow?

IRINA. Eleven years. But why are you crying, Masha, you queer girl? ... (*through her tears*) I shall cry too....

MASHA. I am all right. And in which street did you live?

VERSHININ. In Old Basmanny.

OLGA. And that's where we lived too....

VERSHININ. At one time I lived in Nyemetsky Street. I used to go from there to the Red Barracks. There is a gloomy-looking bridge on the way, where the water makes a noise. It makes a lonely man feel melancholy (*a pause*). And here what a broad, splendid river! A marvellous river!

OLGA. Yes, but it is cold. It's cold here and there are gnats....

VERSHININ. How can you! You've such a splendid healthy Russian climate here. Forest, river ... and birches here too. Charming, modest birches, I love them better than any other trees. It's nice to live here. The only strange thing is that the railway station is fifteen miles away.... And no one knows why it is so.

SOLYONY. I know why it is. (*They all look at him.*) Because if the station had been near it would not have been so far, and if it is far, it's because it is not near.

(*An awkward silence.*)

TUSENBACH. He is fond of his joke, Vassily Vassilyevitch.

OLGA. Now I recall you, too. I remember.

VERSHININ. I knew your mother.

TCHEBUTYKIN. She was a fine woman, the Kingdom of Heaven be hers.

IRINA. Mother is buried in Moscow.

OLGA. In the Novo-Dyevitchy....

MASHA. Would you believe it, I am already beginning to forget her face. So people will not remember us either ... they will forget us.

VERSHININ. Yes. They will forget us. Such is our fate, there is no help for it. What seems to us serious, significant, very important, will one day be forgotten or will seem unimportant (*a pause*). And it's curious that we can't possibly tell what exactly will be considered great and important, and what will seem paltry and ridiculous. Did not the discoveries of Copernicus or Columbus, let us say, seem useless and ridiculous at first, while the nonsensical writings of some wiseacre seemed true? And it may be that our present life, which we accept so readily, will in time seem queer, uncomfortable, not sensible, not clean enough, perhaps even sinful....

TUSENBACH. Who knows? Perhaps our age will be called a great one and remembered with respect. Now we have no torture-chamber, no executions, no invasions, but at the same time how much unhappiness there is!

SOLYONY (*in a high-pitched voice*). Chook, chook, chook.... It's bread and meat to the baron to talk about ideas.

TUSENBACH. Vassily Vassilyevitch, I ask you to let me alone ... (*moves to another seat*). It gets boring, at last.

SOLYONY (*in a high-pitched voice*). Chook, chook, chook....

TUSENBACH (*to* VERSHININ). The unhappiness which one observes now—there is so much of it—does indicate, however, that society has reached a certain moral level....

VERSHININ. Yes, yes, of course.

TCHEBUTYKIN. You said just now, baron, that our age will be called great; but people are small all the same ... (*gets up*). Look how small I am.

(*A violin is played behind the scenes.*)

MASHA. That's Andrey playing, our brother.

IRINA. He is the learned one of the family. We expect him to become a professor. Father was a military man, but his son has gone in for a learned career.

MASHA. It was father's wish.

OLGA. We have been teasing him to-day. We think he is a little in love.

IRINA. With a young lady living here. She will come in to-day most likely.

MASHA. Oh, how she dresses! It's not that her clothes are merely ugly or out of fashion, they are simply pitiful. A queer gaudy yellowish skirt with some sort of vulgar fringe and a red blouse. And her cheeks scrubbed till they shine! Andrey is not in love with her—I won't admit that, he has some taste anyway—it's simply for fun, he is teasing us, playing the fool. I heard yesterday that she is going to be married to Protopopov, the chairman of our Rural Board. And a very good thing too.... (*At the side door*) Andrey, come here, dear, for a minute!

(*Enter* ANDREY.)

OLGA. This is my brother, Andrey Sergeyevitch.

VERSHININ. My name is Vershinin.

ANDREY. And mine is Prozorov (*mops his perspiring face*). You are our new battery commander?

OLGA. Only fancy, Alexandr Ignatyevitch comes from Moscow.

ANDREY. Really? Well, then, I congratulate you. My sisters will let you have no peace.

VERSHININ. I have had time to bore your sisters already.

IRINA. See what a pretty picture-frame Andrey has given me to-day! (*Shows the frame*) He made it himself.

VERSHININ (*looking at the frame and not knowing what to say*). Yes ... it is a thing....

IRINA. And that frame above the piano, he made that too!

(ANDREY *waves his hand in despair and moves away.*)

OLGA. He is learned, and he plays the violin, and he makes all sorts of things with the fretsaw. In fact he is good all round. Andrey, don't go! That's a way he has—he always tries to make off! Come here!

(MASHA *and* IRINA *take him by the arms and, laughing, lead him back.*)

MASHA. Come, come!

ANDREY. Leave me alone, please!

MASHA. How absurd he is! Alexandr Ignatyevitch used to be called the love-sick major at one time, and he was not a bit offended.

VERSHININ. Not in the least!

MASHA. And I should like to call you the love-sick violinist!

IRINA. Or the love-sick professor!

OLGA. He is in love! Andryusha is in love!

IRINA (*claps her hands*). Bravo, bravo! Encore! Andryusha is in love!

TCHEBUTYKIN (*comes up behind* ANDREY *and puts both arms round his waist*). Nature our hearts for love created! (*Laughs, then sits down and reads the newspaper which he takes out of his pocket.*)

ANDREY. Come, that's enough, that's enough ... (*mops his face*). I haven't slept all night and this morning I don't feel quite myself, as they say. I read till four o'clock and then went to bed, but it was no use. I thought of one thing and another, and then it gets light so early; the sun simply pours into my bedroom. I want while I am here during the summer to translate a book from the English....

VERSHININ. You read English then?

ANDREY. Yes. Our father, the Kingdom of Heaven be his, oppressed us with education. It's absurd and silly, but it must be confessed I began to get fatter after his death, and I have grown too fat in one year, as though a weight had been taken off my body. Thanks to our father we all know English, French and German, and Irina knows Italian too. But what it cost us!

MASHA. In this town to know three languages is an unnecessary luxury! Not even a luxury, but an unnecessary encumbrance, like a sixth finger. We know a great deal that is unnecessary.

VERSHININ. What next! (*Laughs.*) You know a great deal that is unnecessary! I don't think there can be a town so dull and dismal that intelligent and educated people are unnecessary in it. Let us suppose that of the hundred thousand people living in this town, which is, of course, uncultured and behind the times, there are only three of your sort. It goes without saying that you cannot conquer the mass of darkness round you; little by little, as you go on living, you will be lost in the crowd. You will have to give in to it. Life will get the better of you, but still you will not disappear without a trace. After you there may appear perhaps six like you, then twelve and so on until such as you form a majority. In two or three hundred years life on earth will be unimaginably beautiful, marvellous. Man needs such a life and, though he hasn't it yet, he must have a presentiment of it, expect it, dream of it, prepare for it; for that he must see and know more than his father and grandfather (*laughs*). And you complain of knowing a great deal that's unnecessary.

MASHA (*takes off her hat*). I'll stay to lunch.

IRINA (*with a sigh*). All that really ought to be written down....

(ANDREY *has slipped away unobserved.*)

TUSENBACH. You say that after many years life on earth will be beautiful and marvellous. That's true. But in order to have any share, however far off, in it now one must be preparing for it, one must be working....

VERSHININ (*gets up*). Yes. What a lot of flowers you have! (*Looking round*) And delightful rooms. I envy you! I've been knocking about all my life from one wretched lodging to another, always with two chairs and a sofa and stoves which smoke. What I have been lacking all my life is just such flowers ... (*rubs his hands*). But there, it's no use thinking about it!

TUSENBACH. Yes, we must work. I'll be bound you think the German is getting sentimental. But on my honour I am Russian and I can't even speak German. My father belonged to the Orthodox Church ... (*a pause*).

VERSHININ (*walks about the stage*). I often think, what if one were to begin life over again, knowing what one is about! If one life, which has been already lived, were only a rough sketch so to say, and the second were the fair copy! Then, I fancy, every one of us would try before everything not to repeat himself, anyway he would create a different setting for his life; would have a house like this with plenty of light and masses of flowers.... I have a wife and two little girls, my wife is in delicate health and so on and so on, but if I were to begin life over again I would not marry.... No, no!

(*Enter* KULIGIN *in the uniform of a school-master.*)

KULIGIN (*goes up to* IRINA). Dear sister, allow me to congratulate you on your name-day and with all my heart to wish you good health and everything else that one can desire for a girl of your age. And to offer you as a gift this little book (*gives her a book*). The history of our high-school for fifty years, written by myself. An insignificant little book, written because I had nothing better to do, but still you can read it. Good morning, friends. (*To* VERSHININ) My name is Kuligin, teacher in the high-school here. (*To* IRINA) In that book you will find a list of all who have finished their studies in our high-school during the last fifty years. *Feci quod potui, faciant meliora potentes* (*kisses* MASHA).

IRINA. Why, but you gave me a copy of this book at Easter.

KULIGIN (*laughs*). Impossible! If that's so, give it me back, or better still, give it to the Colonel. Please accept it, Colonel. Some day when you are bored you can read it.

VERSHININ. Thank you (*is about to take leave*). I am extremely glad to have made your acquaintance....

OLGA. You are going? No, no!

IRINA. You must stay to lunch with us. Please do.

OLGA. Pray do!

VERSHININ (*bows*). I believe I have chanced on a name-day. Forgive me, I did not know and have not congratulated you ... (*Walks away with* OLGA *into the dining-room.*)

KULIGIN. To-day, gentlemen, is Sunday, a day of rest. Let us all rest and enjoy ourselves each in accordance with our age and our position. The carpets should be taken up for the summer and put away till the winter.... Persian powder or naphthaline.... The Romans were healthy because they knew how to work and they knew how to rest, they had *mens sana in corpore sano*. Their life was moulded into a certain framework. Our headmaster says that the most important thing in every life is its framework.... What loses its framework, comes to an end—and it's the same in our everyday life. (*Puts his arm round* MASHA'S *waist, laughing.*) Masha loves me. My wife loves me. And the window curtains, too, ought to be put away together with the carpets.... To-day I feel cheerful and in the best of spirits. Masha, at four o'clock this afternoon we have to be at the headmaster's. An excursion has been arranged for the teachers and their families.

MASHA. I am not going.

KULIGIN (*grieved*). Dear Masha, why not?

MASHA. We'll talk about it afterwards ... (*Angrily*) Very well, I will go, only let me alone, please ... (*walks away*).

KULIGIN. And then we shall spend the evening at the headmaster's. In spite of the delicate state of his health, that man tries before all things to be sociable. He is an excellent, noble personality. A splendid man. Yesterday, after the meeting, he said to me, "I am tired, Fyodor Ilyitch, I am tired." (*Looks at the clock, then at his watch*) Your clock is seven minutes fast. "Yes," he said, "I am tired."

(*Sounds of a violin behind the scenes.*)

OLGA. Come to lunch, please. There's a pie!

KULIGIN. Ah, Olga, my dear Olga! Yesterday I was working from early morning till eleven o'clock at night and was tired out, and to-day I feel happy (*goes up to the table in the dining-room*). My dear....

TCHEBUTYKIN (*puts the newspaper in his pocket and combs his beard*). Pie? Splendid!

MASHA (*to* TCHEBUTYKIN, *sternly*). Only mind you don't drink to-day! Do you hear? It's bad for you to drink.

TCHEBUTYKIN. Oh, come, that's a thing of the past. It's two years since I got drunk. (*Impatiently*) But there, my good girl, what does it matter!

MASHA. Anyway, don't you dare to drink. Don't dare. (*Angrily, but so as not to be heard by her husband*) Again, damnation take it, I am to be bored a whole evening at the headmaster's!

TUSENBACH. I wouldn't go if I were you.... It's very simple.

TCHEBUTYKIN. Don't go, my love.

MASHA. Oh, yes, don't go!... It's a damnable life, insufferable ... (*goes to the dining-room*).

TCHEBUTYKIN (*following her*). Come, come....

SOLYONY (*going to the dining-room*). Chook, chook, chook....

TUSENBACH. Enough, Vassily Vassilyevitch! Leave off!

SOLYONY. Chook, chook, chook....

KULIGIN (*gaily*). Your health, Colonel! I am a school-master and one of the family here, Masha's husband.... She is very kind, really, very kind....

VERSHININ. I'll have some of this dark-coloured vodka ... (*drinks*). To your health! (*To* OLGA) I feel so happy with all of you!

(*No one is left in the drawing-room but* IRINA *and* TUSENBACH.)

IRINA. Masha is in low spirits to-day. She was married at eighteen, when she thought him the cleverest of men. But now it's not the same. He is the kindest of men, but he is not the cleverest.

OLGA (*impatiently*). Andrey, do come!

ANDREY (*behind the scenes*). I am coming (*comes in and goes to the table*).

TUSENBACH. What are you thinking about?

IRINA. Nothing. I don't like that Solyony of yours, I am afraid of him. He keeps on saying such stupid things....

TUSENBACH. He is a queer man. I am sorry for him and annoyed by him, but more sorry. I think he is shy.... When one is alone with him he is very intelligent and friendly, but in company he is rude, a bully. Don't go yet, let them sit down to the table. Let me be by you. What are you thinking of? (*A pause.*) You are twenty, I am not yet thirty. How many years have we got before us, a long, long chain of days full of my love for you....

IRINA. Nikolay Lvovitch, don't talk to me about love.

TUSENBACH (*not listening*). I have a passionate craving for life, for struggle, for work, and that craving is mingled in my soul with my love for you, Irina, and just because you are beautiful it seems to me that life too is beautiful! What are you thinking of?

IRINA. You say life is beautiful.... Yes, but what if it only seems so! Life for us three sisters has not been beautiful yet, we have been stifled by it as plants are choked by weeds.... I am shedding tears.... I mustn't do that (*hurriedly wipes her eyes and smiles*). I must work, I must work. The reason we are depressed and take such a gloomy view of life is that we know nothing of work. We come of people who despised work....

(*Enter* NATALYA IVANOVNA; *she is wearing a pink dress with a green sash.*)

NATASHA. They are sitting down to lunch already.... I am late ... (*Steals a glance at herself in the glass and sets herself to rights*) I think my hair is all right. (*Seeing* IRINA) Dear Irina Sergeyevna, I congratulate you! (*Gives her a vigorous and prolonged kiss.*) You have a lot of visitors, I really feel shy.... Good day, Baron!

OLGA (*coming into the drawing-room*). Well, here is Natalya Ivanovna! How are you, my dear? (*Kisses her.*)

NATASHA. Congratulations on the name-day. You have such a big party and I feel awfully shy....

OLGA. Nonsense, we have only our own people. (*In an undertone, in alarm*) You've got on a green sash! My dear, that's not nice!

NATASHA. Why, is that a bad omen?

OLGA. No, it's only that it doesn't go with your dress ... and it looks queer....

NATASHA (*in a tearful voice*). Really? But you know it's not green exactly, it's more a dead colour (*follows* OLGA *into the dining-room*).

(*In the dining-room they are all sitting down to lunch; there is no one in the drawing-room.*)

KULIGIN. I wish you a good husband, Irina. It's time for you to think of getting married.

TCHEBUTYKIN. Natalya Ivanovna, I hope we may hear of your engagement, too.

KULIGIN. Natalya Ivanovna has got a suitor already.

MASHA (*strikes her plate with her fork*). Ladies and gentlemen, I want to make a speech!

KULIGIN. You deserve three bad marks for conduct.

VERSHININ. How nice this cordial is! What is it made of?

SOLYONY. Beetles.

IRINA (*in a tearful voice*). Ugh, ugh! How disgusting.

OLGA. We are going to have roast turkey and apple pie for supper. Thank God I am at home all day and shall be at home in the evening.... Friends, won't you come this evening?

VERSHININ. Allow me to come too.

IRINA. Please do.

NATASHA. They don't stand on ceremony.

TCHEBUTYKIN. Nature our hearts for love created! (*Laughs*)

ANDREY (*angrily*). Do leave off, I wonder you are not tired of it!

(FEDOTIK *and* RODDEY *come in with a big basket of flowers.*)

FEDOTIK. I say, they are at lunch already.

RODDEY (*speaking loudly, with a lisp*). At lunch? Yes, they are at lunch already....

FEDOTIK. Wait a minute (*takes a snapshot*). One! Wait another minute ... (*takes another snapshot*). Two! Now it's ready. (*They take the basket and walk into the dining-room, where they are greeted noisily.*)

RODDEY (*loudly*). My congratulations! I wish you everything, everything! The weather is delightful, perfectly magnificent. I've been out all the morning for a walk with the high-school boys. I teach them gymnastics.

FEDOTIK. You may move, Irina Sergeyevna, you may move (*taking a photograph*). You look charming to-day (*taking a top out of his pocket*). Here is a top, by the way.... It has a wonderful note....

IRINA. How lovely!

MASHA. By the sea-shore an oak-tree green.... Upon that oak a chain of gold ... (*Complainingly*) Why do I keep saying that? That phrase has been haunting me all day....

KULIGIN. Thirteen at table!

RODDEY (*loudly*). Surely you do not attach importance to such superstitions? (*Laughter.*)

KULIGIN. If there are thirteen at table, it means that someone present is in love. It's not you, Ivan Romanovitch, by any chance? (*Laughter.*)

TCHEBUTYKIN. I am an old sinner, but why Natalya Ivanovna is overcome, I can't imagine ...

(*Loud laughter;* NATASHA *runs out from the dining-room into the drawing-room followed by* ANDREY.)

ANDREY. Come, don't take any notice! Wait a minute ... stop, I entreat you....

NATASHA. I am ashamed.... I don't know what's the matter with me and they make fun of me. I know it's improper for me to leave the table like this, but I can't help it.... I can't ... (*covers her face with her hands*).

ANDREY. My dear girl, I entreat you, I implore you, don't be upset. I assure you they are only joking, they do it in all kindness. My dear, my sweet, they are all kind, warm-hearted people and they are fond of me and of you. Come here to the window, here they can't see us ... (*looks round*).

NATASHA. I am so unaccustomed to society!...

ANDREY. Oh youth, lovely, marvellous youth! My dear, my sweet, don't be so distressed! Believe me, believe me.... I feel so happy, my soul is full of love and rapture.... Oh, they can't see us, they can't see us! Why, why, I love you, when I first loved you—oh, I don't know. My dear, my sweet, pure one, be my wife! I love you, I love you ... as I have never loved anyone ... (*a kiss*).

(*Two officers come in and, seeing the pair kissing, stop in amazement.*)

CURTAIN.

ACT II

The same scene as in the First Act. Eight o'clock in the evening. Behind the scenes in the street there is the faintly audible sound of a concertina. There is no light. NATALYA IVANOVNA enters in a dressing-gown, carrying a candle; she comes in and stops at the door leading to ANDREY's room.

NATASHA. What are you doing, Andryusha? Reading? Never mind, I only just asked ... (*goes and opens another door and, peeping into it, shuts it again*). Is there a light?

ANDREY (*enters with a book in his hand*). What is it, Natasha?

NATASHA. I was looking to see whether there was a light.... It's Carnival, the servants are not themselves; one has always to be on the lookout for fear something goes wrong. Last night at twelve o'clock I passed through the dining-room, and there was a candle left burning. I couldn't find out who had lighted it (*puts down the candle*). What's the time?

ANDREY (*looking at his watch*). A quarter past eight.

NATASHA. And Olga and Irina aren't in yet. They haven't come in. Still at work, poor dears! Olga is at the teachers' council and Irina at the telegraph office ... (*sighs*). I was saying to your sister this morning, "Take care of yourself, Irina darling," said I. But she won't listen. A quarter past eight, you say? I am afraid our Bobik is not at all well. Why is he so cold? Yesterday he was feverish and to-day he is cold all over.... I am so anxious!

ANDREY. It's all right, Natasha. The boy is quite well.

NATASHA. We had better be careful about his food, anyway. I am anxious. And I am told that the mummers are going to be here for the Carnival at nine o'clock this evening. It would be better for them not to come, Andryusha.

ANDREY. I really don't know. They've been invited, you know.

NATASHA. Baby woke up this morning, looked at me, and all at once he gave a smile; so he knew me. "Good morning, Bobik!" said I. "Good morning, darling!" And he laughed. Children understand; they understand very well. So I shall tell them, Andryusha, not to let the carnival party come in.

ANDREY (*irresolutely*). That's for my sisters to say. It's for them to give orders.

NATASHA. Yes, for them too; I will speak to them. They are so kind ... (*is going*). I've ordered junket for supper. The doctor says you must eat nothing but junket, or you will never get thinner (*stops*). Bobik is cold. I am afraid his room is chilly, perhaps. We ought to put him in a different room till the warm weather comes, anyway. Irina's room, for instance, is just right for a nursery: it's dry and the sun shines there all day. I must tell her; she might share Olga's room for the time.... She is never at home, anyway, except for the night ... (*a pause*). Andryushantchik, why don't you speak?

ANDREY. Nothing. I was thinking.... Besides, I have nothing to say.

NATASHA. Yes ... what was it I meant to tell you? ... Oh, yes; Ferapont has come from the Rural Board, and is asking for you.

ANDREY (*yawns*). Send him in.

(NATASHA *goes out;* ANDREY, *bending down to the candle which she has left behind, reads. Enter* FERAPONT; *he wears an old shabby overcoat, with the collar turned up, and has a scarf over his ears.*)

ANDREY. Good evening, my good man. What is it?

FERAPONT. The Chairman has sent a book and a paper of some sort here ... (*gives the book and an envelope*).

ANDREY. Thanks. Very good. But why have you come so late? It is past eight.

FERAPONT. Eh?

ANDREY (*louder*). I say, you have come late. It is eight o'clock.

FERAPONT. Just so. I came before it was dark, but they wouldn't let me see you. The master is busy, they told me. Well, of course, if you are busy, I am in no hurry (*thinking that* ANDREY *has asked him a question*). Eh?

ANDREY. Nothing (*examines the book*). To-morrow is Friday. We haven't a sitting, but I'll come all the same ... and do my work. It's dull at home ... (*a pause*). Dear old man, how strangely life changes and deceives one! To-day I was so bored and had nothing to do, so I picked up this book—old university lectures—and I laughed.... Good heavens! I am the secretary of the Rural Board of which Protopopov is the chairman. I am the secretary, and the most I can hope for is to become a member of the Board! Me, a member of the local Rural Board, while I dream every night I am professor of the University of Moscow—a distinguished man, of whom all Russia is proud!

FERAPONT. I can't say, sir.... I don't hear well....

ANDREY. If you did hear well, perhaps I should not talk to you. I must talk to somebody, and my wife does not understand me. My sisters I am somehow afraid of—I'm afraid they will laugh at me and make me ashamed.... I don't drink, I am not fond of restaurants, but how I should enjoy sitting at Tyestov's in Moscow at this moment, dear old chap!

FERAPONT. A contractor was saying at the Board the other day that there were some merchants in Moscow eating pancakes; one who ate forty, it seems, died. It was either forty or fifty, I don't remember.

ANDREY. In Moscow you sit in a huge room at a restaurant; you know no one and no one knows you, and at the same time you don't feel a stranger.... But here you know everyone and everyone knows you, and yet you are a stranger—a stranger.... A stranger, and lonely....

FERAPONT. Eh? (*A pause.*) And the same contractor says—maybe it's not true—that there's a rope stretched right across Moscow.

ANDREY. What for?

FERAPONT. I can't say, sir. The contractor said so.

ANDREY. Nonsense (*reads*). Have you ever been in Moscow?

FERAPONT (*after a pause*). No, never. It was not God's will I should (*a pause*). Am I to go?

ANDREY. You can go. Good-bye. (FERAPONT *goes out.*) Good-bye (*reading*). Come to-morrow morning and take some papers here.... Go.... (*a pause*). He has gone (*a ring*). Yes, it is a business ... (*stretches and goes slowly into his own room*).

(*Behind the scenes a nurse is singing, rocking a baby to sleep. Enter* MASHA *and* VERSHININ. *While they are talking a maidservant is lighting a lamp and candles in the dining-room.*)

MASHA. I don't know (*a pause*). I don't know. Of course habit does a great deal. After father's death, for instance, it was a long time before we could get used to having no orderlies in the house. But apart from habit, I think it's a feeling of justice makes me say so. Perhaps it is not so in other places, but in our town the most decent, honourable, and well-bred people are all in the army.

VERSHININ. I am thirsty. I should like some tea.

MASHA (*glancing at the clock*). They will soon be bringing it. I was married when I was eighteen, and I was afraid of my husband because he was a teacher, and I had only just left school. In those days I thought him an awfully learned, clever, and important person. And now it is not the same, unfortunately....

VERSHININ. Yes.... I see....

MASHA. I am not speaking of my husband—I am used to him; but among civilians generally there are so many rude, ill-mannered, badly-brought-up people. Rudeness upsets and distresses me: I am unhappy when I see that a man is not refined, not gentle, not polite enough. When I have to be among the teachers, my husband's colleagues, it makes me quite miserable.

VERSHININ. Yes.... But, to my mind, it makes no difference whether they are civilians or military men—they are equally uninteresting, in this town anyway. It's all the same! If one listens to a man of the educated class here, civilian or military, he is worried to death by his wife, worried to death by his house, worried to death by his estate, worried to death by his horses.... A Russian is peculiarly given to exalted ideas, but why is it he always falls so short in life? Why?

MASHA. Why?

VERSHININ. Why is he worried to death by his children and by his wife? And why are his wife and children worried to death by him?

MASHA. You are rather depressed this evening.

VERSHININ. Perhaps.... I've had no dinner to-day, and had nothing to eat since the morning. My daughter is not quite well, and when my little girls are ill I am consumed by anxiety; my conscience reproaches me for having given them such a mother. Oh, if you had seen her to-day! She is a wretched creature! We began quarrelling at seven o'clock in the morning, and at nine I slammed the door and went away (*a pause*). I never talk about it. Strange, it's only to you I complain (*kisses her hand*). Don't be angry with me.... Except for you I have no one—no one ... (*a pause*).

MASHA. What a noise in the stove! Before father died there was howling in the chimney. There, just like that.

VERSHININ. Are you superstitious?

MASHA. Yes.

VERSHININ. That's strange (*kisses her hand*). You are a splendid, wonderful woman. Splendid! Wonderful! It's dark, but I see the light in your eyes.

MASHA (*moves to another chair*). It's lighter here.

VERSHININ. I love you—love, love.... I love your eyes, your movements, I see them in my dreams.... Splendid, wonderful woman!

MASHA (*laughing softly*). When you talk to me like that, for some reason I laugh, though I am frightened.... Please don't do it again ... (*In an undertone*) You may say it, though; I don't mind ... (*covers her face with her hands*). I don't mind.... Someone is coming. Talk of something else.

(IRINA *and* TUSENBACH *come in through the dining-room.*)

TUSENBACH. I've got a three-barrelled name. My name is Baron Tusenbach-Krone-Altschauer, but I belong to the Orthodox Church and am just as Russian as you. There is very little of the German left in me—nothing, perhaps, but the patience and perseverance with which I bore you. I see you home every evening.

IRINA. How tired I am!

TUSENBACH. And every day I will come to the telegraph office and see you home. I'll do it for ten years, for twenty years, till you drive me away ... (*Seeing* MASHA *and* VERSHININ, *delightedly*) Oh, it's you! How are you?

IRINA. Well, I am home at last. (*To* MASHA) A lady came just now to telegraph to her brother in Saratov that her son died to-day, and she could not think of the address. So she sent it without an address—simply to Saratov. She was crying. And I was rude to her for no sort of reason. Told her I had no time to waste. It was so stupid. Are the Carnival people coming to-night?

MASHA. Yes.

IRINA (*sits down in an arm-chair*). I must rest. I am tired.

TUSENBACH (*with a smile*). When you come from the office you seem so young, so forlorn ... (*a pause*).

IRINA. I am tired. No, I don't like telegraph work, I don't like it.

MASHA. You've grown thinner ... (*whistles*). And you look younger, rather like a boy in the face.

TUSENBACH. That's the way she does her hair.

IRINA. I must find some other job, this does not suit me. What I so longed for, what I dreamed of is the very thing that it's lacking in.... It is work without poetry, without meaning.... (*a knock on the floor*). There's the doctor knocking.... (*To* TUSENBACH) Do knock, dear.... I can't.... I am tired.

(TUSENBACH *knocks on the floor.*)

IRINA. He will come directly. We ought to do something about it. The doctor and our Andrey were at the Club yesterday and they lost again. I am told Andrey lost two hundred roubles.

MASHA (*indifferently*). Well, it can't be helped now.

IRINA. A fortnight ago he lost money, in December he lost money. I wish he'd make haste and lose everything, then perhaps we should go away from this town. My God, every night I dream of Moscow, it's perfect madness (*laughs*). We'll move there in June and there is still left February, March, April, May ... almost half a year.

MASHA. The only thing is Natasha must not hear of his losses.

IRINA. I don't suppose she cares.

(TCHEBUTYKIN, *who has only just got off his bed—he has been resting after dinner—comes into the dining-room combing his beard, then sits down to the table and takes a newspaper out of his pocket.*)

MASHA. Here he is ... has he paid his rent?

IRINA (*laughs*). No. Not a kopek for eight months. Evidently he has forgotten.

MASHA (*laughs*). How gravely he sits. (*They all laugh; a pause.*)

IRINA. Why are you so quiet, Alexandr Ignatyevitch?

VERSHININ. I don't know. I am longing for tea. I'd give half my life for a glass of tea. I have had nothing to eat since the morning.

TCHEBUTYKIN. Irina Sergeyevna!

IRINA. What is it?

TCHEBUTYKIN. Come here. *Venez ici.* (IRINA *goes and sits down at the table.*) I can't do without you. (IRINA *lays out the cards for patience.*)

VERSHININ. Well, if they won't bring tea, let us discuss something.

TUSENBACH. By all means. What?

VERSHININ. What? Let us dream ... for instance of the life that will come after us, in two or three hundred years.

TUSENBACH. Well? When we are dead, men will fly in balloons, change the fashion of their coats, will discover a sixth sense, perhaps, and develop it, but life will remain just the same, difficult, full of mysteries and happiness. In a thousand years man will sigh just the same, "Ah, how hard life is," and yet just as now he will be afraid of death and not want it.

VERSHININ (*after a moment's thought*). Well, I don't know.... It seems to me that everything on earth is bound to change by degrees and is already changing before our eyes. In two or three hundred, perhaps in a thousand years—the time does not matter—a new, happy life will come. We shall have no share in that life, of course, but we are living for it, we are working, well, yes, and suffering for it, we are creating it—and that alone is the purpose of our existence, and is our happiness, if you like.

(MASHA *laughs softly.*)

TUSENBACH. What is it?

MASHA. I don't know. I've been laughing all day.

VERSHININ. I was at the same school as you were, I did not go to the Military Academy; I read a great deal, but I do not know how to choose my books, and very likely I read quite the wrong things, and yet the longer I live the more I want to know. My hair is turning grey, I am almost an old man, but I know so little, oh so little! But all the same I fancy that I do know and thoroughly grasp what is essential and matters most. And how I should like to make you see that there is no happiness for us, that there ought not to be and will not be.... We must work and work, and happiness is the portion of our remote descendants (*a pause*). If it is not for me, at least it is for the descendants of my descendants....

(FEDOTIK *and* RODDEY *appear in the dining-room; they sit down and sing softly, playing the guitar.*)

TUSENBACH. You think it's no use even dreaming of happiness! But what if I am happy?

VERSHININ. No.

TUSENBACH (*flinging up his hands and laughing*). It is clear we don't understand each other. Well, how am I to convince you?

(MASHA *laughs softly.*)

TUSENBACH (*holds up a finger to her*). Laugh! (*To* VERSHININ) Not only in two or three hundred years but in a million years life will be just the same; it does not change, it remains stationary, following its own laws which we have nothing to do with or which, anyway, we shall never find out. Migratory birds, cranes for instance, fly backwards and forwards, and whatever ideas, great or small, stray through their minds, they will still go on flying just the same without knowing where or why. They fly and will continue to fly, however philosophic they may become; and it doesn't matter how philosophical they are so long as they go on flying....

MASHA. But still there is a meaning?

TUSENBACH. Meaning.... Here it is snowing. What meaning is there in that? (*A pause.*)

MASHA. I think man ought to have faith or ought to seek a faith, or else his life is empty, empty.... To live and not to understand why cranes fly; why children are born; why there are stars in the sky.... One must know what one is living for or else it is all nonsense and waste (*a pause*).

VERSHININ. And yet one is sorry that youth is over....

MASHA. Gogol says: it's dull living in this world, friends!

TUSENBACH. And I say: it is difficult to argue with you, my friends, God bless you....

TCHEBUTYKIN (*reading the newspaper*). Balzac was married at Berditchev.

(IRINA *hums softly.*)

TCHEBUTYKIN. I really must put that down in my book. (*Writes*) Balzac was married at Berditchev (*reads the paper*).

IRINA (*lays out the cards for patience, dreamily*). Balzac was married at Berditchev.

TUSENBACH. The die is cast. You know, Marya Sergeyevna, I've resigned my commission.

MASHA. So I hear. And I see nothing good in that. I don't like civilians.

TUSENBACH. Never mind ... (*gets up*). I am not good-looking enough for a soldier. But that does not matter, though ... I am going to work. If only for one day in my life, to work so that I come home at night tired out and fall asleep as soon as I get into bed ... (*going into the dining-room*). Workmen must sleep soundly!

FEDOTIK (*to* IRINA). I bought these chalks for you just now as I passed the shop.... And this penknife....

IRINA. You've got into the way of treating me as though I were little, but I am grown up, you know ... (*takes the chalks and the penknife, joyfully*). How lovely!

FEDOTIK. And I bought a knife for myself ... look ... one blade, and another blade, a third, and this is for the ears, and here are scissors, and that's for cleaning the nails....

RODDEY (*loudly*). Doctor, how old are you?

TCHEBUTYKIN. I? Thirty-two (*laughter*).

FEDOTIK. I'll show you another patience ... (*lays out the cards*).

(*The samovar is brought in;* ANFISA *is at the samovar; a little later* NATASHA *comes in and is also busy at the table;* SOLYONY *comes in, and after greeting the others sits down at the table.*)

VERSHININ. What a wind there is!

MASHA. Yes. I am sick of the winter. I've forgotten what summer is like.

IRINA. It's coming out right, I see. We shall go to Moscow.

FEDOTIK. No, it's not coming out. You see, the eight is over the two of spades (*laughs*). So that means you won't go to Moscow.

TCHEBUTYKIN (*reads from the newspaper*). Tsi-tsi-kar. Smallpox is raging here.

ANFISA (*going up to* MASHA). Masha, come to tea, my dear. (*To* VERSHININ) Come, your honour ... excuse me, sir, I have forgotten your name....

MASHA. Bring it here, nurse, I am not going there.

IRINA. Nurse!

ANFISA. I am coming!

NATASHA (*to* SOLYONY). Little babies understand very well. "Good morning Bobik, good morning, darling," I said. He looked at me in quite a special way. You think I say that because I am a mother, but no, I assure you! He is an extraordinary child.

SOLYONY. If that child were mine, I'd fry him in a frying-pan and eat him. (*Takes his glass, comes into the drawing-room and sits down in a corner.*)

NATASHA (*covers her face with her hands*). Rude, ill-bred man!

MASHA. Happy people don't notice whether it is winter or summer. I fancy if I lived in Moscow I should not mind what the weather was like....

VERSHININ. The other day I was reading the diary of a French minister written in prison. The minister was condemned for the Panama affair. With what enthusiasm and delight he describes the birds he sees from the prison window, which he never noticed before when he was a minister. Now that he is released, of course he notices birds no more than he did before. In the same way, you won't notice Moscow when you live in it. We have no happiness and never do have, we only long for it.

TUSENBACH (*takes a box from the table*). What has become of the sweets?

IRINA. Solyony has eaten them.

TUSENBACH. All?

ANFISA (*handling tea*). There's a letter for you, sir.

VERSHININ. For me? (*Takes the letter.*) From my daughter (*reads*). Yes, of course.... Excuse me, Marya Sergeyevna, I'll slip away. I won't have tea (*gets up in agitation*). Always these upsets....

MASHA. What is it? Not a secret?

VERSHININ (*in a low voice*). My wife has taken poison again. I must go. I'll slip off unnoticed. Horribly unpleasant it all is. (*Kisses* MASHA's *hand*) My fine, dear, splendid woman.... I'll go this way without being seen ... (*goes out*).

ANFISA. Where is he off to? I've just given him his tea.... What a man.

MASHA (*getting angry*). Leave off! Don't pester, you give one no peace ... (*goes with her cup to the table*). You bother me, old lady.

ANFISA. Why are you so huffy? Darling!

(*Andrey's voice:* "ANFISA!")

ANFISA (*mimicking*). Anfisa! He sits there ... (*goes out*).

MASHA (*by the table in the dining-room, angrily*). Let me sit down! (*Mixes the cards on the table.*) You take up all the table with your cards. Drink your tea!

IRINA. How cross you are, Masha!

MASHA. If I'm cross, don't talk to me. Don't interfere with me.

TCHEBUTYKIN (*laughing*). Don't touch her, don't touch her!

MASHA. You are sixty, but you talk rot like a schoolboy.

NATASHA (*sighs*). Dear Masha, why make use of such expressions in conversation? With your attractive appearance I tell you straight out, you would be simply fascinating in a well-bred social circle if it were not for the things you say. *Je vous prie, pardonnez-moi, Marie, mais vous avez des manières un peu grossières.*

TUSENBACH (*suppressing a laugh*). Give me ... give me ... I think there is some brandy there.

NATASHA. *Il paraît que mon Bobik déjà ne dort pas,* he is awake. He is not well to-day. I must go to him, excuse me ... (*goes out*).

IRINA. Where has Alexandr Ignatyevitch gone?

MASHA. Home. Something queer with his wife again.

TUSENBACH (*goes up to* SOLYONY *with a decanter of brandy in his hand*). You always sit alone, thinking, and there's no making out what you think about. Come, let us make it up. Let us have a drink of brandy. (*They drink.*) I shall have to play the piano all night, I suppose, play all sorts of trash.... Here goes!

SOLYONY. Why make it up? I haven't quarrelled with you.

TUSENBACH. You always make me feel as though something had gone wrong between us. You are a queer character, there's no denying that.

SOLYONY (*declaims*). I am strange, who is not strange! Be not wrath, Aleko!

TUSENBACH. I don't see what Aleko has got to do with it....

SOLYONY. When I am *tête-à-tête* with somebody, I am all right, just like anyone else, but in company I am depressed, ill at ease and ... say all sorts of idiotic things, but at the same time I am more conscientious and straightforward than many. And I can prove it....

TUSENBACH. I often feel angry with you, you are always attacking me when we are in company, and yet I somehow like you. Here goes, I am going to drink a lot to-day. Let's drink!

SOLYONY. Let us (*drinks*). I have never had anything against you, Baron. But I have the temperament of Lermontov. (*In a low voice*) In fact I am rather like Lermontov to look at ... so I am told (*takes out scent-bottle and sprinkles scent on his hands*).

TUSENBACH. I have sent in my papers. I've had enough of it! I have been thinking of it for five years and at last I have come up to the scratch. I am going to work.

SOLYONY (*declaims*). Be not wrath, Aleko.... Forget, forget thy dreams....

(*While they are talking* ANDREY *comes in quietly with a book and sits down by a candle.*)

TUSENBACH. I am going to work.

TCHEBUTYKIN (*coming into the drawing-room with* IRINA). And the food too was real Caucasian stuff: onion soup and for the meat course *tchehartma*....

SOLYONY. *Tcheremsha* is not meat at all, it's a plant rather like our onion.

TCHEBUTYKIN. No, my dear soul, it's not onion, but mutton roasted in a special way.

SOLYONY. But I tell you that *tcheremsha* is an onion.

TCHEBUTYKIN. And I tell you that *tchehartma* is mutton.

SOLYONY. And I tell you that *tcheremsha* is an onion.

TCHEBUTYKIN. What's the use of my arguing with you? You have never been to the Caucasus or eaten *tchehartma*.

SOLYONY. I haven't eaten it because I can't bear it. *Tcheremsha* smells like garlic.

ANDREY (*imploringly*). That's enough! Please!

TUSHENBACH. When are the Carnival party coming?

IRINA. They promised to come at nine, so they will be here directly.

TUSENBACH (*embraces* ANDREY *and sings*). "Oh my porch, oh my new porch ..."

ANDREY (*dances and sings*). "With posts of maple wood...."

TCHEBUTYKIN (*dances*). "And lattice work complete ..." (*laughter*).

TUSENBACH (*kisses* ANDREY). Hang it all, let us have a drink. Andryusha, let us drink to our everlasting friendship. I'll go to the University when you do, Andryusha.

SOLYONY. Which? There are two universities in Moscow.

ANDREY. There is only one university in Moscow.

SOLYONY. I tell you there are two.

ANDREY. There may be three for aught I care. So much the better.

SOLYONY. There are two universities in Moscow! (*A murmur and hisses.*) There are two universities in Moscow: the old one and the new one. And if you don't care to hear, if what I say irritates you, I can keep quiet. I can even go into another room (*goes out at one of the doors*).

TUSENBACH. Bravo, bravo! (*Laughs.*) Friends, begin, I'll sit down and play! Funny fellow that Solyony.... (*Sits down to the piano and plays a waltz.*)

MASHA (*dances a waltz alone*). The baron is drunk, the baron is drunk, the baron is drunk.

(*Enter* NATASHA.)

NATASHA (*to* TCHEBUTYKIN). Ivan Romanitch! (*Says something to* TCHEBUTYKIN, *then goes out softly.* TCHEBUTYKIN *touches* TUSENBACH *on the shoulder and whispers something to him.*)

IRINA. What is it?

TCHEBUTYKIN. It's time we were going. Good night.

TUSENBACH. Good night. It's time to be going.

IRINA. But I say ... what about the Carnival party?

ANDREY (*with embarrassment*). They won't be coming. You see, dear, Natasha says Bobik is not well, and so ... In fact I know nothing about it, and don't care either.

IRINA (*shrugs her shoulders*). Bobik is not well!

MASHA. Well, it's not the first time we've had to lump it! If we are turned out, we must go. (*To* IRINA) It's not Bobik that is ill, but she is a bit ... (*taps her forehead with her finger*). Petty, vulgar creature!

(ANDREY *goes by door on right to his own room*, TCHEBUTYKIN *following him; they are saying good-bye in the dining-room.*)

FEDOTIK. What a pity! I was meaning to spend the evening, but of course if the child is ill ... I'll bring him a toy to-morrow.

RODDEY (*loudly*). I had a nap to-day after dinner on purpose, I thought I would be dancing all night.... Why, it's only nine o'clock.

MASHA. Let us go into the street; there we can talk. We'll decide what to do.

(*Sounds of* "Good-bye! Good night!" *The good-humoured laugh of* TUSEN-BACH *is heard. All go out.* ANFISA *and the maidservant clear the table and put out the light. There is the sound of the nurse singing.* ANDREY *in his hat and coat, and* TCHEBUTYKIN *come in quietly.*)

TCHEBUTYKIN. I never had time to get married, because life has flashed by like lightning and because I was passionately in love with your mother, who was married.

ANDREY. One shouldn't get married. One shouldn't, because it's boring.

TCHEBUTYKIN. That's all very well, but what about loneliness? Say what you like, it's a dreadful thing to be lonely, my dear boy.... But no matter, though!

ANDREY. Let's make haste and go.

TCHEBUTYKIN. What's the hurry? We have plenty of time.

ANDREY. I am afraid my wife may stop me.

TCHEBUTYKIN. Oh!

ANDREY. I am not going to play to-day, I shall just sit and look on. I don't feel well.... What am I to do, Ivan Romanitch, I am so short of breath?

TCHEBUTYKIN. It's no use asking me! I don't remember, dear boy.... I don't know....

ANDREY. Let us go through the kitchen. (*They go out.*)

(*A ring, then another ring; there is a sound of voices and laughter.*)

IRINA (*enters*). What is it?

ANFISA (*in a whisper*). The mummers, all dressed up (*a ring*).

IRINA. Nurse, dear, say there is no one at home. They must excuse us.

(ANFISA *goes out.* IRINA *walks about the room in hesitation; she is excited. Enter* SOLYONY.)

SOLYONY (*in perplexity*). No one here.... Where are they all?

IRINA. They have gone home.

SOLYONY. How queer. Are you alone here?

IRINA. Yes (*a pause*). Good night.

SOLYONY. I behaved tactlessly, without sufficient restraint just now. But you are not like other people, you are pure and lofty, you see the truth. You alone can understand me. I love you, I love you deeply, infinitely.

IRINA. Good night! You must go.

SOLYONY. I can't live without you (*following her*). Oh, my bliss! (*Through his tears*) Oh, happiness! Those glorious, exquisite, marvellous eyes such as I have never seen in any other woman.

IRINA (*coldly*). Don't, Vassily Vassilyitch!

SOLYONY. For the first time I am speaking of love to you, and I feel as though I were not on earth but on another planet (*rubs his forehead*). But there, it does not matter. There is no forcing kindness, of course.... But there must be no happy rivals.... There must not.... I swear by all that is sacred I will kill any rival.... O exquisite being!

(NATASHA *passes with a candle.*)

NATASHA (*peeps in at one door, then at another and passes by the door that leads to her husband's room*). Andrey is there. Let him read. Excuse me, Vassily Vassilyitch, I did not know you were here, and I am in my dressing-gown....

SOLYONY. I don't care. Good-bye! (*Goes out.*)

NATASHA. You are tired, my poor, dear little girl! (*Kisses* IRINA.) You ought to go to bed earlier....

IRINA. Is Bobik asleep?

NATASHA. He is asleep, but not sleeping quietly. By the way, dear, I keep meaning to speak to you, but either you are out or else I haven't the time.... I think Bobik's nursery is cold and damp. And your room is so nice for a baby. My sweet, my dear, you might move for a time into Olya's room!

IRINA (*not understanding*). Where?

(*The sound of a three-horse sledge with bells driving up to the door.*)

NATASHA. You would be in the same room with Olya, and Bobik in your room. He is such a poppet. I said to him to-day, "Bobik, you are mine, you are mine!" and he looked at me with his funny little eyes. (*A ring.*) That must be Olya. How late she is!

(*The maid comes up to* NATASHA *and whispers in her ear.*)

NATASHA. Protopopov? What a queer fellow he is! Protopopov has come, and asks me to go out with him in his sledge (*laughs*). How strange men are!... (*A ring*) Somebody has come. I might go for a quarter of an hour.... (*To the maid*) Tell him I'll come directly. (*A ring*) You hear ... it must be Olya (*goes out*).

(*The maid runs out;* IRINA *sits lost in thought;* KULIGIN, OLGA *and* VERSHININ *come in.*)

KULIGIN. Well, this is a surprise! They said they were going to have an evening party.

VERSHININ. Strange! And when I went away half an hour ago they were expecting the Carnival people....

IRINA. They have all gone.

KULIGIN. Has Masha gone too? Where has she gone? And why is Protopopov waiting below with his sledge? Whom is he waiting for?

IRINA. Don't ask questions.... I am tired.

KULIGIN. Oh, you little cross-patch....

OLGA. The meeting is only just over. I am tired out. Our headmistress is ill and I have to take her place. Oh, my head, my head does ache;

oh, my head! (*Sits down.*) Andrey lost two hundred roubles yester-day at cards.... The whole town is talking about it....

KULIGIN. Yes, I am tired out by the meeting too (*sits down*).

VERSHININ. My wife took it into her head to give me a fright, she nearly poisoned herself. It's all right now, and I'm glad, it's a re-lief.... So we are to go away? Very well, then, I will say good night. Fyodor Ilyitch, let us go somewhere together! I can't stay at home, I absolutely can't.... Come along!

KULIGIN. I am tired. I am not coming (*gets up*). I am tired. Has my wife gone home?

IRINA. I expect so.

KULIGIN (*kisses* IRINA's *hand*). Good-bye! I have all day to-morrow and next day to rest. Good night! (*Going*) I do want some tea. I was reck-oning on spending the evening in pleasant company.... *O fallacem hominum spem!*... Accusative of exclamation.

VERSHININ. Well, then, I must go alone (*goes out with* KULIGIN, *whistling*).

OLGA. My head aches, oh, how my head aches.... Andrey has lost at cards.... The whole town is talking about it.... I'll go and lie down (*is going*). To-morrow I shall be free.... Oh, goodness, how nice that is! To-morrow I am free, and the day after I am free.... My head does ache, oh, my head ... (*goes out*).

IRINA (*alone*). They have all gone away. There is no one left.

(*A concertina plays in the street, the nurse sings.*)

NATASHA (*in a fur cap and coat crosses the dining-room, followed by the maid*). I shall be back in half an hour. I shall only go a little way (*goes out*).

IRINA (*left alone, in dejection*). Oh, to go to Moscow, to Moscow!

CURTAIN.

ACT III

The Bedroom of OLGA *and* IRINA. *On left and right beds with screens round them. Past two o'clock in the night. Behind the scenes a bell is ringing on account of a fire in the town, which has been going on for some time. It can be seen that no one in the house has gone to bed yet. On the sofa* MASHA *is lying, dressed as usual in black. Enter* OLGA *and* ANFISA.

ANFISA. They are sitting below, under the stairs.... I said to them, "Come upstairs; why, you mustn't stay there"—they only cried. "We don't know where father is," they said. "What if he is burnt!" What an idea! And the poor souls in the yard ... they are all undressed too.

OLGA (*taking clothes out of the cupboard*). Take this grey dress ... and this one ... and the blouse too ... and that skirt, nurse.... Oh, dear, what a dreadful thing! Kirsanov Street is burnt to the ground, it seems.... Take this ... take this ... (*throws clothes into her arms*). The Vershinins have had a fright, poor things.... Their house was very nearly burnt. Let them stay the night here ... we can't let them go home.... Poor Fedotik has had everything burnt, he has not a thing left....

ANFISA. You had better call Ferapont, Olya darling, I can't carry it all.

OLGA (*rings*). No one will answer the bell (*at the door*). Come here, whoever is there! (*Through the open door can be seen a window red with fire; the fire brigade is heard passing the house.*) How awful it is! And how sickening!

(*Enter* FERAPONT.)

OLGA. Here take these, carry them downstairs.... The Kolotilin young ladies are downstairs ... give it to them ... and give this too.

FERAPONT. Yes, miss. In 1812 Moscow was burnt too.... Mercy on us! The French marvelled.

OLGA. You can go now.

FERAPONT. Yes, miss (*goes out*).

OLGA. Nurse darling, give them everything. We don't want anything, give it all to them.... I am tired, I can hardly stand on my feet.... We mustn't let the Vershinins go home.... The little girls can sleep in the drawing-room, and Alexandr Ignatyevitch down below at the baron's.... Fedotik can go to the baron's, too, or sleep in our dining-room.... As ill-luck will have it, the doctor is drunk, frightfully drunk, and no one can be put in his room. And Vershinin's wife can be in the drawing-room too.

ANFISA (*wearily*). Olya darling, don't send me away; don't send me away!

OLGA. That's nonsense, nurse. No one is sending you away.

ANFISA (*lays her head on* OLGA's *shoulder*). My own, my treasure, I work, I do my best.... I'm getting weak, everyone will say "Be off!" And where am I to go? Where? I am eighty. Eighty-one.

OLGA. Sit down, nurse darling.... You are tired, poor thing ... (*makes her sit down*). Rest, dear good nurse.... How pale you are!

(*Enter* NATASHA.)

NATASHA. They are saying we must form a committee at once for the assistance of those whose houses have been burnt. Well, that's a good idea. Indeed, one ought always to be ready to help the poor, it's the duty of the rich. Bobik and baby Sophie are both asleep, sleeping as though nothing were happening. There are such a lot of people everywhere, wherever one goes, the house is full. There is influenza in the town now; I am so afraid the children may get it.

OLGA (*not listening*). In this room one does not see the fire, it's quiet here.

NATASHA. Yes ... my hair must be untidy (*in front of the looking-glass*). They say I have grown fatter ... but it's not true! Not a bit! Masha is asleep, she is tired out, poor dear.... (*To* ANFISA *coldly*) Don't dare to sit down in my presence! Get up! Go out of the room! (ANFISA *goes out; a pause.*) Why you keep that old woman, I can't understand!

OLGA (*taken aback*). Excuse me, I don't understand either....

NATASHA. She is no use here. She is a peasant; she ought to be in the country.... You spoil people! I like order in the house! There ought to be no useless servants in the house. (*Strokes her cheek.*) You are tired, poor darling. Our headmistress is tired! When baby Sophie is a big girl and goes to the high-school, I shall be afraid of you.

OLGA. I shan't be headmistress.

NATASHA. You will be elected, Olya. That's a settled thing.

OLGA. I shall refuse. I can't.... It's too much for me ... (*drinks water*). You were so rude to nurse just now.... Excuse me, I can't endure it.... It makes me feel faint.

NATASHA (*perturbed*). Forgive me, Olya; forgive me.... I did not mean to hurt your feelings.

(MASHA *gets up, takes her pillow, and goes out in a rage.*)

OLGA. You must understand, my dear, it may be that we have been strangely brought up, but I can't endure it.... Such an attitude oppresses me, it makes me ill.... I feel simply unnerved by it....

NATASHA. Forgive me; forgive me ... (*kisses her*).

OLGA. The very slightest rudeness, a tactless word, upsets me....

NATASHA. I often say too much, that's true, but you must admit, dear, that she might just as well be in the country.

OLGA. She has been thirty years with us.

NATASHA. But now she can't work! Either I don't understand, or you won't understand me. She is not fit for work. She does nothing but sleep or sit still.

OLGA. Well, let her sit still.

NATASHA (*surprised*). How, sit still? Why, she is a servant. (*Through tears*) I don't understand you, Olya. I have a nurse to look after the children as well as a wet nurse for baby, and we have a housemaid and a cook, what do we want that old woman for? What's the use of her?

(*The alarm bell rings behind the scenes.*)

OLGA. This night has made me ten years older.

NATASHA. We must come to an understanding, Olya. You are at the high-school, I am at home; you are teaching while I look after the house, and if I say anything about the servants, I know what I'm talking about; I do know what I am talking about.... And that old thief, that old hag ... (*stamps*), that old witch shall clear out of the house to-morrow!... I won't have people annoy me! I won't have it! (*Feeling that she has gone too far*) Really, if you don't move downstairs, we shall always be quarrelling. It's awful.

(*Enter* KULIGIN.)

KULIGIN. Where is Masha? It's time to be going home. The fire is dying down, so they say (*stretches*). Only one part of the town has been burnt, and yet there was a wind; it seemed at first as though the whole town would be destroyed (*sits down*). I am exhausted. Olya, my dear ... I often think if it had not been for Masha I should have married you. You are so good.... I am tired out (*listens*).

OLGA. What is it?

KULIGIN. It is unfortunate the doctor should have a drinking bout just now; he is helplessly drunk. Most unfortunate (*gets up*). Here he comes, I do believe.... Do you hear? Yes, he is coming this way ... (*laughs*). What a man he is, really.... I shall hide (*goes to the cupboard and stands in the corner*). Isn't he a ruffian!

OLGA. He has not drunk for two years and now he has gone and done it ... (*walks away with* NATASHA *to the back of the room*).

(TCHEBUTYKIN *comes in; walking as though sober without staggering, he walks across the room, stops, looks round; then goes up to the washing-stand and begins to wash his hands.*)

TCHEBUTYKIN (*morosely*). The devil take them all ... damn them all. They think I am a doctor, that I can treat all sorts of complaints, and I really know nothing about it, I have forgotten all I did know, I remember nothing, absolutely nothing. (OLGA *and* NATASHA *go out unnoticed by him.*) The devil take them. Last Wednesday I treated a woman at Zasyp—she died, and it's my fault that she died. Yes ... I did know something twenty-five years ago, but now I remember nothing, nothing. Perhaps I am not a man at all but only pretend to have arms and legs and head; perhaps I don't exist at all and only fancy that I walk about, eat and sleep (*weeps*). Oh, if only I did not exist! (*Leaves off weeping, morosely*) I don't care! I don't care a scrap! (*A pause.*) Goodness knows.... The day before yesterday there was a conversation at the club: they talked about Shakespeare, Voltaire.... I have read nothing, nothing at all, but I looked as though I had read them. And the others did the same as I did. The vulgarity! The meanness! And that woman I killed on Wednesday came back to my mind ... and it all came back to my mind and everything seemed nasty, disgusting and all awry in my soul.... I went and got drunk....

(*Enter* IRINA, VERSHININ *and* TUSENBACH; TUSENBACH *is wearing a fashionable new civilian suit.*)

IRINA. Let us sit here. No one will come here.

VERSHININ. If it had not been for the soldiers, the whole town would have been burnt down. Splendid fellows! (*Rubs his hands with pleasure.*) They are first-rate men! Splendid fellows!

KULIGIN (*going up to them*). What time is it?

TUSENBACH. It's past three. It's getting light already.

IRINA. They are all sitting in the dining-room. No one seems to think of going. And that Solyony of yours is sitting there too.... (*To* TCHEBUTYKIN) You had better go to bed, doctor.

TCHEBUTYKIN. It's all right.... Thank you! (*Combs his beard.*)

KULIGIN (*laughs*). You are a bit fuddled, Ivan Romanitch! (*Slaps him on the shoulder.*) Bravo! *In vino veritas,* the ancients used to say.

TUSENBACH. Everyone is asking me to get up a concert for the benefit of the families whose houses have been burnt down.

IRINA. Why, who is there? ...

TUSENBACH. We could get it up, if we wanted to. Marya Sergeyevna plays the piano splendidly, to my thinking.

KULIGIN. Yes, she plays splendidly.

IRINA. She has forgotten. She has not played for three ... or four years.

TUSENBACH. There is absolutely no one who understands music in this town, not one soul, but I do understand and on my honour I assure you that Marya Sergeyevna plays magnificently, almost with genius.

KULIGIN. You are right, Baron. I am very fond of her; Masha, I mean. She is a good sort.

TUSENBACH. To be able to play so gloriously and to know that no one understands you!

KULIGIN (*sighs*). Yes.... But would it be suitable for her to take part in a concert? (*A pause.*) I know nothing about it, my friends. Perhaps it would be all right. There is no denying that our director is a fine man, indeed a very fine man, very intelligent, but he has such views.... Of course it is not his business, still if you like I'll speak to him about it.

(TCHEBUTYKIN *takes up a china clock and examines it.*)

VERSHININ. I got dirty all over at the fire. I am a sight (*a pause*). I heard a word dropped yesterday about our brigade being transferred ever so far away. Some say to Poland, and others to Tchita.

TUSENBACH. I've heard something about it too. Well! The town will be a wilderness then.

IRINA. We shall go away too.

TCHEBUTYKIN (*drops the clock, which smashes*). To smithereens!

KULIGIN (*picking up the pieces*). To smash such a valuable thing—oh, Ivan Romanitch, Ivan Romanitch! I should give you minus zero for conduct!

IRINA. That was mother's clock.

TCHEBUTYKIN. Perhaps.... Well, if it was hers, it was. Perhaps I did not smash it, but it only seems as though I had. Perhaps it only seems to us that we exist, but really we are not here at all. I don't know anything—nobody knows anything. (*By the door*) What are you staring at? Natasha has got a little affair on with Protopopov, and you don't see it.... You sit here and see nothing, while Natasha has a little affair on with Protopopov ... (*Sings.*) May I offer you this date? ... (*Goes out.*)

VERSHININ. Yes ... (*laughs*). How very queer it all is, really! (*A pause.*) When the fire began I ran home as fast as I could. I went up and saw our house was safe and sound and out of danger, but my little girls were standing in the doorway in their nightgowns; their mother was nowhere to be seen, people were bustling about, horses and dogs were running about, and my children's faces were full of alarm, horror, entreaty, and I don't know what; it wrung my heart to see their faces. My God, I thought, what more have these children to go through in the long years to come! I took their hands and ran along with them, and could think of nothing else but what more they would have to go through in this world! (*A pause.*) When I came to your house I found their mother here, screaming, angry.

(MASHA *comes in with the pillow and sits down on the sofa.*)

VERSHININ. And while my little girls were standing in the doorway in their nightgowns and the street was red with the fire, and there was a fearful noise, I thought that something like it used to happen years ago when the enemy would suddenly make a raid and begin plundering and burning.... And yet, in reality, what a difference there is between what is now and has been in the past! And when a little more time has passed—another two or three hundred years—people will look at our present manner of life with horror and derision, and everything of to-day will seem awkward and heavy, and very strange and uncomfortable. Oh, what a wonderful life that will be—what a wonderful life! (*Laughs*) Forgive me, here I am airing my theories again! Allow me to go on. I have such a desire to talk about the future. I am in the mood (*a pause*). It's as though everyone were asleep. And so, I say, what a wonderful life it will be! Can you only imagine?... Here there are only three of your sort in the town now, but in generations to come there will be more and more and more; and the time will come when everything will be changed and be as you would have it; they will live in your way, and later on you too will be out of date—people will be born who will be better than you ... (*laughs*). I am in such a strange state of mind to-day. I have a fiendish longing for life ... (*Sings.*) Young and old are bound by love, and precious are its pangs ... (*laughs*).

MASHA. Tram-tam-tam!

VERSHININ. Tam-tam!

MASHA. Tra-ra-ra?
VERSHININ. Tra-ta-ta! (*Laughs.*)

(*Enter* FEDOTIK.)

FEDOTIK (*dances*). Burnt to ashes! Burnt to ashes! Everything I had in the world (*laughter*).
IRINA. A queer thing to joke about. Is everything burnt?
FEDOTIK (*laughs*). Everything I had in the world. Nothing is left. My guitar is burnt, and the camera and all my letters.... And the note-book I meant to give you—that's burnt too.

(*Enter* SOLYONY.)

IRINA. No; please go, Vassily Vassilyitch. You can't stay here.
SOLYONY. How is it the baron can be here and I can't?
VERSHININ. We must be going, really. How is the fire?
SOLYONY. They say it is dying down. No, I really can't understand why the baron may be here and not I (*takes out a bottle of scent and sprinkles himself*).
VERSHININ. Tram-tam-tam!
MASHA. Tram-tam!
VERSHININ (*laughs, to* SOLYONY). Let us go into the dining-room.
SOLYONY. Very well; we'll make a note of it. I might explain my meaning further, but fear I may provoke the geese ... (*looking at* TUSENBACH). Chook, chook, chook!... (*Goes out with* VERSHININ *and* FEDOTIK.)
IRINA. How that horrid Solyony has made the room smell of to-bacco!... (*In surprise*) The baron is asleep! Baron, baron!
TUSENBACH (*waking up*). I am tired, though.... The brickyard. I am not talking in my sleep. I really am going to the brickyard directly, to begin work.... It's nearly settled. (*To* IRINA, *tenderly*) You are so pale and lovely and fascinating.... It seems to me as though your pale-ness sheds a light through the dark air.... You are melancholy; you are dissatisfied with life.... Ah, come with me; let us go and work together!
MASHA. Nikolay Lvovitch, do go!

TUSENBACH (*laughing*). Are you here? I didn't see you ... (*kisses* IRINA'S *hand*). Good-bye, I am going.... I look at you now, and I remember as though it were long ago how on your name-day you talked of the joy of work, and were so gay and confident.... And what a happy life I was dreaming of then! What has become of it? (*Kisses her hand.*) There are tears in your eyes. Go to bed, it's getting light ... it is nearly morning.... If it were granted to me to give my life for you!

MASHA. Nikolay Lvovitch, do go! Come, really....

TUSENBACH. I am going (*goes out*).

MASHA (*lying down*). Are you asleep, Fyodor?

KULIGIN. Eh?

MASHA. You had better go home.

KULIGIN. My darling Masha, my precious girl!...

IRINA. She is tired out. Let her rest, Fedya.

KULIGIN. I'll go at once.... My dear, charming wife!... I love you, my only one!...

MASHA (*angrily*). *Amo, amas, amat; amamus, amatis, amant.*

KULIGIN (*laughs*). Yes, really she is wonderful. You have been my wife for seven years, and it seems to me as though we were only married yesterday. Honour bright! Yes, really you are a wonderful woman! I am content, I am content, I am content!

MASHA. I am bored, I am bored, I am bored!... (*Gets up and speaks, sitting down*) And there's something I can't get out of my head.... It's simply revolting. It sticks in my head like a nail; I must speak of it. I mean about Andrey.... He has mortgaged this house in the bank and his wife has grabbed all the money, and you know the house does not belong to him alone, but to us four! He ought to know that, if he is a decent man.

KULIGIN. Why do you want to bother about it, Masha? What is it to you? Andryusha is in debt all round, so there it is.

MASHA. It's revolting, anyway (*lies down*).

KULIGIN. We are not poor. I work—I go to the high-school, and then I give private lessons.... I do my duty.... There's no nonsense about me. *Omnia mea mecum porto,* as the saying is.

MASHA. I want nothing, but it's the injustice that revolts me (*a pause*). Go, Fyodor.

KULIGIN (*kisses her*). You are tired, rest for half an hour, and I'll sit and wait for you.... Sleep ... (*goes*). I am content, I am content, I am content (*goes out*).

IRINA. Yes, how petty our Andrey has grown, how dull and old he has become beside that woman! At one time he was working to get a professorship and yesterday he was boasting of having succeeded at last in becoming a member of the Rural Board. He is a member, and Protopopov is chairman.... The whole town is laughing and talking of it and he is the only one who sees and knows nothing.... And here everyone has been running to the fire while he sits still in his room and takes no notice. He does nothing but play his violin.... (*Nervously*) Oh, it's awful, awful, awful! (*Weeps*) I can't bear it any more, I can't! I can't, I can't!

(OLGA *comes in and begins tidying up her table.*)

IRINA (*sobs loudly*). Turn me out, turn me out, I can't bear it any more!

OLGA (*alarmed*). What is it? What is it, darling?

IRINA (*sobbing*). Where? Where has it all gone? Where is it? Oh, my God, my God! I have forgotten everything, everything ... everything is in a tangle in my mind.... I don't remember the Italian for window or ceiling ... I am forgetting everything; every day I forget something more and life is slipping away and will never come back, we shall never, never go to Moscow.... I see that we shan't go....

OLGA. Darling, darling....

IRINA (*restraining herself*). Oh, I am wretched.... I can't work, I am not going to work. I have had enough of it, enough of it! I have been a telegraph clerk and now I have a job in the town council and I hate and despise every bit of the work they give me.... I am nearly twenty-four, I have been working for years, my brains are drying up, I am getting thin and old and ugly and there is nothing, nothing, not the slightest satisfaction, and time is passing and one feels that one is moving away from a real, fine life, moving farther and farther away and being drawn into the depths. I am in despair and I don't know how it is I am alive and have not killed myself yet....

OLGA. Don't cry, my child, don't cry. It makes me miserable.

IRINA. I am not crying, I am not crying.... It's over.... There, I am not crying now. I won't ... I won't.

OLGA. Darling, I am speaking to you as a sister, as a friend, if you care for my advice, marry the baron!

(IRINA *weeps.*)

OLGA (*softly*). You know you respect him, you think highly of him.... It's true he is ugly, but he is such a thoroughly nice man, so good.... One doesn't marry for love, but to do one's duty.... That's what I think, anyway, and I would marry without love. Whoever proposed to me I would marry him, if only he were a good man.... I would even marry an old man....

IRINA. I kept expecting we should move to Moscow and there I should meet my real one. I've been dreaming of him, loving him.... But it seems that was all nonsense, nonsense....

OLGA (*puts her arms round her sister*). My darling, lovely sister, I under-stand it all; when the baron left the army and came to us in a plain coat, I thought he looked so ugly that it positively made me cry.... He asked me, "Why are you crying?" How could I tell him! But if God brought you together I should be happy. That's a different thing, you know, quite different.

(NATASHA *with a candle in her hand walks across the stage from door on right to door on left without speaking.*)

MASHA (*sits up*). She walks about as though it were she had set fire to the town.

OLGA. Masha, you are silly. The very silliest of the family, that's you. Please forgive me (*a pause*).

MASHA. I want to confess my sins, dear sisters. My soul is yearning. I am going to confess to you and never again to anyone.... I'll tell you this minute (*softly*). It's my secret, but you must know everything.... I can't be silent ... (*a pause*). I am in love, I am in love.... I love that man.... You have just seen him.... Well, I may as well say it straight out. I love Vershinin.

OLGA (*going behind her screen*). Leave off. I don't hear anyway.

MASHA. But what am I to do? (*Clutches her head.*) At first I thought him queer ... then I was sorry for him ... then I came to love him ... to love him with his voice, his words, his misfortunes, his two little girls....

OLGA (*behind the screen*). I don't hear you anyway. Whatever silly things you say I shan't hear them.

MASHA. Oh, Olya, you are silly. I love him—so that's my fate. It means that that's my lot.... And he loves me.... It's all dreadful. Yes? Is it wrong? (*Takes* IRINA *by the hand and draws her to herself.*) Oh, my darling.... How are we going to live our lives, what will become of us?... When one reads a novel it all seems stale and easy to understand, but when you are in love yourself you see that no one knows anything and we all have to settle things for ourselves.... My darling, my sister.... I have confessed it to you, now I'll hold my tongue.... I'll be like Gogol's madman ... silence ... silence....

(*Enter* ANDREY *and after him* FERAPONT.)

ANDREY (*angrily*). What do you want? I can't make it out.

FERAPONT (*in the doorway, impatiently*). I've told you ten times already, Andrey Sergeyevitch.

ANDREY. In the first place I am not Andrey Sergeyevitch, but your honour, to you!

FERAPONT. The firemen ask leave, your honour, to go through the garden on their way to the river. Or else they have to go round and round, an awful nuisance for them.

ANDREY. Very good. Tell them, very good. (FERAPONT *goes out.*) I am sick of them. Where is Olga? (OLGA *comes from behind the screen.*) I've come to ask you for the key of the cupboard, I have lost mine. You've got one, it's a little key.

(OLGA *gives him the key in silence;* IRINA *goes behind her screen; a pause.*)

ANDREY. What a tremendous fire! Now it's begun to die down. Hang it all, that Ferapont made me so cross I said something silly to him. Your honour ... (*a pause*). Why don't you speak, Olya? (*A pause.*) It's time to drop this foolishness and sulking all about nothing.... You are here, Masha, and you too, Irina—very well, then, let us have things out thoroughly, once for all. What have you against me? What is it?

OLGA. Leave off, Andryusha. Let us talk to-morrow. (*Nervously*) What an agonising night!

ANDREY (*greatly confused*). Don't excite yourself. I ask you quite coolly, what have you against me? Tell me straight out.

(VERSHININ'S *voice:* "Tram-tam-tam!")

MASHA (*standing up, loudly*). Tra-ta-ta! (*To* OLGA) Good night, Olya, God bless you … (*Goes behind the screen and kisses* IRINA.) Sleep well…. Good night, Andrey. You'd better leave them now, they are tired out … you can go into things to-morrow (*goes out*).

OLGA. Yes, really, Andryusha, let us put it off till to-morrow … (*goes behind her screen*). It's time we were in bed.

ANDREY. I'll say what I have to say and then go. Directly…. First, you have something against Natasha, my wife, and I've noticed that from the very day of my marriage. Natasha is a splendid woman, conscientious, straightforward and honourable—that's my opinion! I love and respect my wife, do you understand? I respect her, and I insist on other people respecting her too. I repeat, she is a conscientious, honourable woman, and all your disagreements are simply caprice, or rather the whims of old maids. Old maids never like and never have liked their sisters-in-law—that's the rule (*a pause*). Secondly, you seem to be cross with me for not being a professor, not working at something learned. But I am in the service of the Zemstvo, I am a member of the Rural Board, and I consider this service just as sacred and elevated as the service of learning. I am a member of the Rural Board and I am proud of it, if you care to know … (*a pause*). Thirdly … there's something else I have to say…. I have mortgaged the house without asking your permission…. For that I am to blame, yes, and I ask your pardon for it. I was driven to it by my debts … thirty-five thousand…. I am not gambling now— I gave up cards long ago; but the chief thing I can say in self-defence is that you are, so to say, of the privileged sex—you get a pension … while I had not … my wages, so to speak … (*a pause*).

KULIGIN (*at the door*). Isn't Masha here? (*Perturbed*) Where is she? It's strange ... (*goes out*).

ANDREY. They won't listen. Natasha is an excellent, conscientious woman (*paces up and down the stage in silence, then stops*). When I married her, I thought we should be happy ... happy, all of us.... But, my God! (*Weeps*) Dear sisters, darling sisters, you must not believe what I say, you mustn't believe it ... (*goes out*).

KULIGIN (*at the door, uneasily*). Where is Masha? Isn't Masha here? How strange! (*Goes out.*)

(*The firebell rings in the street. The stage is empty.*)

IRINA (*behind the screen*). Olya! Who is that knocking on the floor?

OLGA. It's the doctor, Ivan Romanitch. He is drunk.

IRINA. What a troubled night! (*A pause.*) Olya! (*Peeps out from behind the screen.*) Have you heard? The brigade is going to be taken away; they are being transferred to some place very far off.

OLGA. That's only a rumour.

IRINA. Then we shall be alone.... Olya!

OLGA. Well?

IRINA. My dear, my darling, I respect the baron, I think highly of him, he is a fine man—I will marry him, I consent, only let us go to Moscow! I entreat you, do let us go! There's nothing in the world better than Moscow! Let us go Olya! Let us go!

CURTAIN.

ACT IV

Old garden of the PROZOROVS' *house. A long avenue of fir trees, at the end of which is a view of the river. On the farther side of the river there is a wood. On the right the verandah of the house; on the table in it are bottles and glasses; evidently they have just been drinking champagne. It is twelve o'clock in the day. People pass occasionally from the street across the garden to the river; five soldiers pass rapidly.*

TCHEBUTYKIN, *in an affable mood, which persists throughout the act, is sitting in an easy chair in the garden, waiting to be summoned; he is wearing a military cap and has a stick.* IRINA, KULIGIN *with a decoration on his breast and with no moustache, and* TUSENBACH, *standing on the verandah, are saying good-bye to* FEDOTIK *and* RODDEY, *who are going down the steps; both officers are in marching uniform.*

TUSENBACH (*kissing* FEDOTIK). You are a good fellow; we've got on so happily together. (*Kisses* RODDEY.) Once more.... Good-bye, my dear boy....

IRINA. Till we meet again!

FEDOTIK. No, it's good-bye for good; we shall never meet again.

KULIGIN. Who knows! (*Wipes his eyes, smiles.*) Here I am crying too.

IRINA. We shall meet some day.

FEDOTIK. In ten years, or fifteen perhaps? But then we shall scarcely recognise each other—we shall greet each other coldly ... (*Takes a snapshot*) Stand still.... Once more, for the last time.

RODDEY (*embraces* TUSENBACH). We shall not see each other again.... (*Kisses* IRINA's *hand.*) Thank you for everything, everything....

FEDOTIK (*with vexation*). Oh, do wait!

TUSENBACH. Please God we shall meet again. Write to us. Be sure to write to us.

RODDEY (*taking a long look at the garden*). Good-bye, trees! (*Shouts*) Halloo! (*A pause.*) Good-bye, echo!

KULIGIN. I shouldn't wonder if you get married in Poland.... Your Polish wife will clasp you in her arms and call you *kochany*! (*Laughs.*)

FEDOTIK (*looking at his watch*). We have less than an hour. Of our battery only Solyony is going on the barge; we are going with the rank and file. Three divisions of the battery are going to-day and three more to-morrow—and peace and quiet will descend upon the town.

TUSENBACH. And dreadful boredom too.

RODDEY. And where is Marya Sergeyevna?

KULIGIN. Masha is in the garden.

FEDOTIK. We must say good-bye to her.

RODDEY. Good-bye. We must go, or I shall begin to cry ... (*Hurriedly embraces* TUSENBACH *and* KULIGIN *and kisses* IRINA'*s hand.*) We've had a splendid time here.

FEDOTIK (*to* KULIGIN). This is a little souvenir for you ... a note-book with a pencil.... We'll go down here to the river ... (*As they go away both look back.*)

RODDEY (*shouts*). Halloo-oo!

KULIGIN (*shouts*). Good-bye!

(RODDEY *and* FEDOTIK *meet* MASHA *in the background and say good-bye to her; she walks away with them.*)

IRINA. They've gone ... (*Sits down on the bottom step of the verandah.*)

TCHEBUTYKIN. They have forgotten to say good-bye to me.

IRINA. And what were you thinking about?

TCHEBUTYKIN. Why, I somehow forget, too. But I shall see them again soon, I am setting off to-morrow. Yes ... I have one day more. In a year I shall be on the retired list. Then I shall come here again and shall spend the rest of my life near you.... There is only one year now before I get my pension. (*Puts a newspaper into his pocket and takes out another.*) I shall come here to you and arrange my life quite differently.... I shall become such a quiet ... God-fearing ... well-behaved person.

IRINA. Well, you do need to arrange your life differently, dear Ivan Romanitch. You certainly ought to somehow.

TCHEBUTYKIN. Yes, I feel it. (*Softly hums*) "Tarara-boom-dee-ay—Tarara-boom-dee-ay."

KULIGIN. Ivan Romanitch is incorrigible! Incorrigible!

TCHEBUTYKIN. You ought to take me in hand. Then I should reform.

IRINA. Fyodor has shaved off his moustache. I can't bear to look at him!

KULIGIN. Why, what's wrong?

TCHEBUTYKIN. I might tell you what your countenance looks like now, but I really can't.

KULIGIN. Well! It's the thing now, *modus vivendi*. Our headmaster is clean-shaven and now I am second to him I have taken to shaving too. Nobody likes it, but I don't care. I am content. With moustache or without moustache I am equally content (*sits down*).

(*In the background* ANDREY *is wheeling a baby asleep in a perambulator.*)

IRINA. Ivan Romanitch, darling, I am dreadfully uneasy. You were on the boulevard yesterday, tell me what was it that happened?

TCHEBUTYKIN. What happened? Nothing. Nothing much (*reads the newspaper*). It doesn't matter!

KULIGIN. The story is that Solyony and the baron met yesterday on the boulevard near the theatre....

TUSENBACH. Oh, stop it! Really ... (*with a wave of his hand walks away into the house*).

KULIGIN. Near the theatre.... Solyony began pestering the baron and he couldn't keep his temper and said something offensive....

TCHEBUTYKIN. I don't know. It's all nonsense.

KULIGIN. A teacher at a divinity school wrote "nonsense" at the bottom of an essay and the pupil puzzled over it thinking it was a Latin word ... (*laughs*). It was fearfully funny.... They say Solyony is in love with Irina and hates the baron.... That's natural. Irina is a very nice girl.

(*From the background behind the scenes,* "Aa-oo! Halloo!")

IRINA (*starts*). Everything frightens me somehow to-day (*a pause*). All my things are ready, after dinner I shall send off my luggage. The baron and I are to be married to-morrow, to-morrow we go to the brickyard and the day after that I shall be in the school. A new life is beginning. God will help me! How will it fare with me? When I passed my exam as a teacher, I felt so happy, so blissful, that I cried ... (*a pause*). The cart will soon be coming for my things....

KULIGIN. That's all very well, but it does not seem serious. It's all nothing but ideas and very little that is serious. However, I wish you success with all my heart.

TCHEBUTYKIN (*moved to tenderness*). My good, delightful darling.... My heart of gold....

KULIGIN. Well, to-day the officers will be gone and everything will go on in the old way. Whatever people may say, Masha is a true, good woman. I love her dearly and am thankful for my lot! ... People have different lots in life.... There is a man called Kozyrev serving in the Excise here. He was at school with me, but he was expelled from the fifth form because he could never understand *ut consecutivum*. Now he is frightfully poor and ill, and when I meet him I say, "How are you, *ut consecutivum*?" "Yes," he says, "just so— *consecutivum*" ... and then he coughs.... Now, I have always been successful, I am fortunate, I have even got the order of the Stanislav of the second degree and I am teaching others that *ut consecutivum*. Of course I am clever, cleverer than very many people, but happiness does not lie in that ... (*a pause*).

(*In the house the "Maiden's Prayer" is played on the piano.*)

IRINA. To-morrow evening I shall not be hearing that "Maiden's Prayer," I shan't be meeting Protopopov ... (*a pause*). Protopopov is sitting there in the drawing-room; he has come again to-day....

KULIGIN. The headmistress has not come yet?

IRINA. No. They have sent for her. If only you knew how hard it is for me to live here alone, without Olya.... Now that she is headmistress and lives at the high-school and is busy all day long, I am alone, I am bored, I have nothing to do, and I hate the room I live in.... I have made up my mind, since I am not fated to be in Moscow, that so it must be. It must be destiny. There is no help for it.... It's all in God's hands, that's the truth. When Nikolay Lvovitch made me an offer again ... I thought it over and made up my mind.... He is a good man, it's wonderful really how good he is.... And I suddenly felt as though my soul had grown wings, my heart felt so light and again I longed for work, work.... Only something happened yesterday, there is some mystery hanging over me.

TCHEBUTYKIN. Nonsense.

NATASHA (*at the window*). Our headmistress!

KULIGIN. The headmistress has come. Let us go in (*goes into the house with* IRINA).

TCHEBUTYKIN (*reads the newspaper, humming softly*). "Tarara-boom-dee-ay."

(MASHA *approaches; in the background* ANDREY *is pushing the perambulator.*)

MASHA. Here he sits, snug and settled.

TCHEBUTYKIN. Well, what then?

MASHA (*sits down*). Nothing ... (*a pause*). Did you love my mother?

TCHEBUTYKIN. Very much.

MASHA. And did she love you?

TCHEBUTYKIN (*after a pause*). That I don't remember.

MASHA. Is my man here? It's just like our cook Marfa used to say about her policeman: is my man here?

TCHEBUTYKIN. Not yet.

MASHA. When you get happiness by snatches, by little bits, and then lose it, as I am losing it, by degrees one grows coarse and spiteful ... (*Points to her bosom*) I'm boiling here inside ... (*Looking at* ANDREY, *who is pushing the perambulator*) Here is our Andrey.... All our hopes are shattered. Thousands of people raised the bell, a lot of money and of labour was spent on it, and it suddenly fell and smashed. All at once, for no reason whatever. That's just how it is with Andrey....

ANDREY. When will they be quiet in the house? There is such a noise.

TCHEBUTYKIN. Soon (*looks at his watch*). My watch is an old-fashioned one with a repeater ... (*winds his watch, it strikes*). The first, the second, and the fifth batteries are going at one o'clock (*a pause*). And I am going to-morrow.

ANDREY. For good?

TCHEBUTYKIN. I don't know. Perhaps I shall come back in a year. Though goodness knows.... It doesn't matter one way or another.

(*There is the sound of a harp and violin being played far away in the street.*)

ANDREY. The town will be empty. It's as though one put an extinguisher over it (*a pause*). Something happened yesterday near the theatre; everyone is talking of it, and I know nothing about it.

TCHEBUTYKIN. It was nothing. Foolishness. Solyony began annoying the baron and he lost his temper and insulted him, and it came in the end to Solyony's having to challenge him (*looks at his watch*). It's time, I fancy.... It was to be at half-past twelve in the Crown forest that we can see from here beyond the river ... Piff-paff! (*Laughs*) Solyony imagines he is a Lermontov and even writes verses. Joking apart, this is his third duel.

MASHA. Whose?

TCHEBUTYKIN. Solyony's.

MASHA. And the baron's?

TCHEBUTYKIN. What about the baron? (*A pause.*)

MASHA. My thoughts are in a muddle.... Anyway, I tell you, you ought not to let them do it. He may wound the baron or even kill him.

TCHEBUTYKIN. The baron is a very good fellow, but one baron more or less in the world, what does it matter? Let them! It doesn't matter. (*Beyond the garden a shout of* "Aa-oo! Halloo!") You can wait. That is Skvortsov, the second, shouting. He is in a boat (*a pause*).

ANDREY. In my opinion to take part in a duel, or to be present at it even in the capacity of a doctor, is simply immoral.

TCHEBUTYKIN. That only seems so.... We are not real, nothing in the world is real, we don't exist, but only seem to exist.... Nothing matters!

MASHA. How they keep on talking, talking all day long (*goes*). To live in such a climate, it may snow any minute, and then all this talk on the top of it (*stops*). I am not going indoors, I can't go in there.... When Vershinin comes, tell me ... (*goes down the avenue*). And the birds are already flying south ... (*looks up*). Swans or geese.... Darlings, happy things ... (*goes out*).

ANDREY. Our house will be empty. The officers are going, you are going, Irina is getting married, and I shall be left in the house alone.

TCHEBUTYKIN. What about your wife?

(*Enter* FERAPONT *with papers.*)

ANDREY. A wife is a wife. She is a straightforward, upright woman, good-natured, perhaps, but for all that there is something in her which makes her no better than some petty, blind, hairy animal. Anyway she is not a human being. I speak to you as to a friend, the one man to whom I can open my soul. I love Natasha, that is so, but sometimes she seems to me wonderfully vulgar, and then I don't know what to think, I can't account for my loving her or, anyway, having loved her.

TCHEBUTYKIN (*gets up*). I am going away to-morrow, my boy, perhaps we shall never meet again, so this is my advice to you. Put on your cap, you know, take your stick and walk off ... walk off and just go, go without looking back. And the farther you go, the better (*a pause*). But do as you like! It doesn't matter....

(SOLYONY *crosses the stage in the background with two officers; seeing* TCHEBUTYKIN *he turns towards him; the officers walk on.*)

SOLYONY. Doctor, it's time! It's half-past twelve (*greets* ANDREY).

TCHEBUTYKIN. Directly. I am sick of you all. (*To* ANDREY) If any-one asks for me, Andryusha, say I'll be back directly ... (*sighs*). Oho-ho-ho!

SOLYONY. He had not time to say alack before the bear was on his back (*walks away with the doctor*). Why are you croaking, old chap?

TCHEBUTYKIN. Come!

SOLYONY. How do you feel?

TCHEBUTYKIN (*angrily*). Like a pig in clover.

SOLYONY. The old chap need not excite himself. I won't do anything much, I'll only shoot him like a snipe (*takes out scent and sprinkles his hands*). I've used a whole bottle to-day, and still they smell. My hands smell like a corpse (*a pause*). Yes.... Do you remember the poem? "And, restless, seeks the stormy ocean, as though in tempest there were peace." ...

TCHEBUTYKIN. Yes. He had not time to say alack before the bear was on his back. (*Goes out with* SOLYONY. *Shouts are heard:* "Halloo! Oo-oo!" ANDREY *and* FERAPONT *come in.*)

FERAPONT. Papers for you to sign....

ANDREY (*nervously*). Let me alone! Let me alone! I entreat you! (*Walks away with the perambulator.*)

FERAPONT. That's what the papers are for—to be signed (*retires into the background*).

(*Enter* IRINA *and* TUSENBACH *wearing a straw hat;* KULIGIN *crosses the stage shouting* "Aa-oo, Masha, aa-oo!")

TUSENBACH. I believe that's the only man in the town who is glad that the officers are going away.

IRINA. That's very natural (*a pause*). Our town will be empty now.

TUSENBACH. Dear, I'll be back directly.

IRINA. Where are you going?

TUSENBACH. I must go into the town, and then ... to see my comrades off.

IRINA. That's not true.... Nikolay, why are you so absent-minded to-day? (*A pause.*) What happened yesterday near the theatre?

TUSENBACH (*with a gesture of impatience*). I'll be here in an hour and with you again (*kisses her hands*). My beautiful one ... (*looks into her face*). For five years now I have loved you and still I can't get used to it, and you seem to me more and more lovely. What wonderful, exquisite hair! What eyes! I shall carry you off to-morrow, we will work, we will be rich, my dreams will come true. You shall be happy. There is only one thing, one thing: you don't love me!

IRINA. That's not in my power! I'll be your wife and be faithful and obedient, but there is no love, I can't help it (*weeps*). I've never been in love in my life! Oh, I have so dreamed of love, I've been dreaming of it for years, day and night, but my soul is like a wonderful piano of which the key has been lost (*a pause*). You look uneasy.

TUSENBACH. I have not slept all night. There has never been anything in my life so dreadful that it could frighten me, and only that lost key frets at my heart and won't let me sleep.... Say something to me ... (*a pause*). Say something to me....

IRINA. What? What am I to say to you? What?

TUSENBACH. Anything.

IRINA. There, there! (*A pause.*)

TUSENBACH. What trifles, what little things suddenly *à propos* of nothing acquire importance in life! One laughs at them as before, thinks them nonsense, but still one goes on and feels that one has not the power to stop. Don't let us talk about it! I am happy. I feel as though I were seeing these pines, these maples, these birch trees for the first time in my life, and they all seem to be looking at me with curiosity and waiting. What beautiful trees, and, really, how beautiful life ought to be under them! (*A shout of* "Halloo! Aa-oo!") I must be off; it's time.... See, that tree is dead, but it waves in the wind with the others. And so it seems to me that if I die I shall still have part in life, one way or another. Good-bye, my darling ... (*kisses her hands*). Those papers of yours you gave me are lying under the calendar on my table.

IRINA. I am coming with you.

TUSENBACH (*in alarm*). No, no! (*Goes off quickly, stops in the avenue.*) Irina!

IRINA. What is it?

TUSENBACH (*not knowing what to say*). I didn't have any coffee this morning. Ask them to make me some (*goes out quickly*).

(IRINA *stands lost in thought, then walks away into the background of the scene and sits down on the swing. Enter* ANDREY *with the perambulator, and* FERAPONT *comes into sight.*)

FERAPONT. Andrey Sergeyevitch, the papers aren't mine; they are Government papers. I didn't invent them.

ANDREY. Oh, where is it all gone? What has become of my past, when I was young, gay, and clever, when my dreams and thoughts were exquisite, when my present and my past were lighted up by hope? Why on the very threshold of life do we become dull, grey, uninteresting, lazy, indifferent, useless, unhappy? ... Our town has been going on for two hundred years—there are a hundred thousand people living in it; and there is not one who is not like the rest, not one saint in the past, or the present, not one man of learning, not one artist, not one man in the least remarkable who could inspire envy or a passionate desire to imitate him.... They only eat, drink, sleep, and then die ... others are born, and they also eat and drink and sleep, and not to be bored to stupefaction they vary their lives by nasty gossip, vodka, cards, litigation; and the wives deceive their husbands, and the husbands tell lies and pretend that they see and hear nothing, and an overwhelmingly vulgar influence weighs upon the children, and the divine spark is quenched in them and they become the same sort of pitiful, dead creatures, all exactly alike, as their fathers and mothers.... (*To* FERAPONT, *angrily*) What do you want?

FERAPONT. Eh? There are papers to sign.

ANDREY. You bother me!

FERAPONT (*handing him the papers*). The porter from the local treasury was saying just now that there was as much as two hundred degrees of frost in Petersburg this winter.

ANDREY. The present is hateful, but when I think of the future, it is so nice! I feel so light-hearted, so free. A light dawns in the distance, I see freedom. I see how I and my children will become free from sloth, from kvass, from goose and cabbage, from sleeping after dinner, from mean, parasitic living....

FERAPONT. He says that two thousand people were frozen to death. The people were terrified. It was either in Petersburg or Moscow, I don't remember.

ANDREY (*in a rush of tender feeling*). My dear sisters, my wonderful sisters! (*Through tears*) Masha, my sister!

NATASHA (*in the window*). Who is talking so loud out there? Is that you, Andryusha? You will wake baby Sophie. *Il ne faut pas faire de bruit, la Sophie est dormée déjà. Vous êtes un ours.* (*Getting angry*) If you want to talk, give the perambulator with the baby to somebody else. Ferapont, take the perambulator from the master!

FERAPONT. Yes, ma'am (*takes the pram*).

ANDREY (*in confusion*). I am talking quietly.

NATASHA (*petting her child, inside the room*). Bobik! Naughty Bobik! Little rascal!

ANDREY (*looking through the papers*). Very well, I'll look through them and sign what wants signing, and then you can take them back to the Board.... (*Goes into the house reading the papers;* FERAPONT *pushes the pram farther into the garden.*)

NATASHA (*speaking indoors*). Bobik, what is mamma's name? Darling, darling! And who is this? This is auntie Olya. Say to auntie, "Good morning, Olya!"

(*Two wandering musicians, a man and a girl, enter and play a violin and a harp; from the house enter* VERSHININ *with* OLGA *and* ANFISA, *and stand for a minute listening in silence;* IRINA *comes up.*)

OLGA. Our garden is like a public passage; they walk and ride through. Nurse, give those people something.

ANFISA (*gives money to the musicians*). Go away, and God bless you, my dear souls! (*The musicians bow and go away.*) Poor things. People don't play if they have plenty to eat. (*To* IRINA) Good morning, Irisha! (*Kisses her.*) Aye, aye, my little girl, I am having a time of it! Living in the high-school, in a government flat, with dear Olya—that's what the Lord has vouchsafed me in my old age! I have never lived so well in my life, sinful woman that I am.... It's a big flat, and I have a room to myself and a bedstead. All at the government's expense. I wake up in the night and, O Lord, Mother of God, there is no one in the world happier than I!

VERSHININ (*looks at his watch*). We are just going, Olga Sergeyevna. It's time to be off (*a pause*). I wish you everything, everything.... Where is Marya Sergeyevna?

IRINA. She is somewhere in the garden.... I'll go and look for her.

VERSHININ. Please be so good. I am in a hurry.

ANFISA. I'll go and look for her too. (*Shouts*) Mashenka, aa-oo! (*Goes with* IRINA *into the farther part of the garden.*) Aa-oo! Aa-oo!

VERSHININ. Everything comes to an end. Here we are parting (*looks at his watch*). The town has given us something like a lunch; we have been drinking champagne, the mayor made a speech. I ate and listened, but my heart was here, with you all ... (*looks round the garden*). I've grown used to you....

OLGA. Shall we ever see each other again?

VERSHININ. Most likely not (*a pause*). My wife and two little girls will stay here for another two months; please, if anything happens, if they need anything ...

OLGA. Yes, yes, of course. Set your mind at rest (*a pause*). By to-morrow there won't be a soldier in the town—it will all turn into a memory, and of course for us it will be like beginning a new life ... (*a pause*). Nothing turns out as we would have it. I did not want to be a headmistress, and yet I am. It seems we are not to live in Moscow....

VERSHININ. Well.... Thank you for everything.... Forgive me if anything was amiss.... I have talked a great deal: forgive me for that too—don't remember evil against me.

OLGA (*wipes her eyes*). Why doesn't Masha come?

VERSHININ. What else am I to say to you at parting? What am I to theorise about? ... (*Laughs*) Life is hard. It seems to many of us blank and hopeless; but yet we must admit that it goes on getting clearer and easier, and it looks as though the time were not far off when it will be full of happiness (*looks at his watch*). It's time for me to go! In old days men were absorbed in wars, filling all their existence with marches, raids, victories, but now all that is a thing of the past, leaving behind it a great void which there is so far nothing to fill: humanity is searching for it passionately, and of course will find it. Ah, if only it could be quickly! (*A pause.*) If, don't you know, industry were united with culture and culture with industry ... (*Looks at his watch*) But, I say, it's time for me to go....

OLGA. Here she comes.

(MASHA *comes in.*)

VERSHININ. I have come to say good-bye....

(OLGA *moves a little away to leave them free to say good-bye.*)

MASHA (*looking into his face*). Good-bye ... (*a prolonged kiss*).

OLGA. Come, come....

(MASHA *sobs violently.*)

VERSHININ. Write to me.... Don't forget me! Let me go! ... Time is up!... Olga Sergeyevna, take her, I must ... go ... I am late ... (*Much moved, kisses* OLGA's *hands; then again embraces* MASHA *and quickly goes off.*)

OLGA. Come, Masha! Leave off, darling.

(*Enter* KULIGIN.)

KULIGIN (*embarrassed*). Never mind, let her cry—let her.... My good Masha, my dear Masha!... You are my wife, and I am happy, anyway.... I don't complain; I don't say a word of blame.... Here Olya is my witness.... We'll begin the old life again, and I won't say one word, not a hint....

MASHA (*restraining her sobs*). By the sea-strand an oak-tree green.... Upon that oak a chain of gold.... Upon that oak a chain of gold.... I am going mad.... By the sea-strand ... an oak-tree green....

OLGA. Calm yourself, Masha.... Calm yourself.... Give her some water.

MASHA. I am not crying now....

KULIGIN. She is not crying now ... she is good....

(*The dim sound of a far-away shot.*)

MASHA. By the sea-strand an oak-tree green, upon that oak a chain of gold.... The cat is green ... the oak is green.... I am mixing it up ... (*drinks water*). My life is a failure.... I want nothing now.... I shall be calm directly.... It doesn't matter.... What does "strand" mean? Why do these words haunt me? My thoughts are in a tangle.

(*Enter* IRINA.)

OLGA. Calm yourself, Masha. Come, that's a good girl. Let us go indoors.

MASHA (*angrily*). I am not going in. Let me alone! (*Sobs, but at once checks herself.*) I don't go into that house now and I won't.

IRINA. Let us sit together, even if we don't say anything. I am going away to-morrow, you know ... (*a pause*).

KULIGIN. I took a false beard and moustache from a boy in the third

form yesterday, just look ... (*puts on the beard and moustache*). I look like the German teacher ... (*laughs*). Don't I? Funny creatures, those boys.
MASHA. You really do look like the German teacher.
OLGA (*laughs*). Yes.

(MASHA *weeps.*)

IRINA. There, Masha!
KULIGIN. Awfully like....

(*Enter* NATASHA.)

NATASHA (*to the maid*). What? Mr. Protopopov will sit with Sophie, and let Andrey Sergeyitch wheel Bobik up and down. What a lot there is to do with children ... (*To* IRINA) Irina, you are going away to-morrow, what a pity. Do stay just another week. (*Seeing* KULIGIN *utters a shriek; the latter laughs and takes off the beard and moustache.*) Well, what next, you gave me such a fright! (*To* IRINA) I am used to you and do you suppose that I don't feel parting with you? I shall put Andrey with his violin into your room—let him saw away there!—and we will put baby Sophie in his room. Adorable, delightful baby! Isn't she a child! To-day she looked at me with such eyes and said "Mamma"!
KULIGIN. A fine child, that's true.
NATASHA. So to-morrow I shall be all alone here (*sighs*). First of all I shall have this avenue of fir trees cut down, and then that maple.... It looks so ugly in the evening.... (*To* IRINA) My dear, that sash does not suit you at all.... It's in bad taste. You want something light. And then I shall have flowers, flowers planted everywhere, and there will be such a scent.... (*Severely*) Why is there a fork lying about on that seat? (*Going into the house, to the maid*) Why is there a fork lying about on this seat. I ask you? (*Shouts*) Hold your tongue!
KULIGIN. She is at it!

(*Behind the scenes the band plays a march; they all listen.*)

OLGA. They are going.

(*Enter* TCHEBUTYKIN.)

MASHA. Our people are going. Well ... a happy journey to them! (*To her husband*) We must go home.... Where are my hat and cape?

KULIGIN. I took them into the house ... I'll get them directly....

OLGA. Yes, now we can go home, it's time.

TCHEBUTYKIN. Olga Sergeyevna!

OLGA. What is it? (*A pause.*) What?

TCHEBUTYKIN. Nothing.... I don't know how to tell you. (*Whispers in her ear.*)

OLGA (*in alarm*). It can't be!

TCHEBUTYKIN. Yes ... such a business.... I am so worried and worn out, I don't want to say another word.... (*With vexation*) But there, it doesn't matter!

MASHA. What has happened?

OLGA (*puts her arms round* IRINA). This is a terrible day.... I don't know how to tell you, my precious....

IRINA. What is it? Tell me quickly, what is it? For God's sake! (*Cries.*)

TCHEBUTYKIN. The baron has just been killed in a duel.

IRINA (*weeping quietly*). I knew, I knew....

TCHEBUTYKIN (*in the background of the scene sits down on a garden seat*). I am worn out ... (*takes a newspaper out of his pocket*). Let them cry.... (*Sings softly*) "Tarara-boom-dee-ay" ... It doesn't matter.

(*The three sisters stand with their arms round one another.*)

MASHA. Oh, listen to that band! They are going away from us; one has gone altogether, gone forever. We are left alone to begin our life over again.... We've got to live ... we've got to live....

IRINA (*lays her head on* OLGA's *bosom*). A time will come when everyone will know what all this is for, why there is this misery; there will be no mysteries and, meanwhile, we have got to live ... we have got to work, only to work! To-morrow I shall go alone; I shall teach in the school, and I will give all my life to those to whom it may be of use. Now it's autumn; soon winter will come and cover us with snow, and I will work, I will work.

OLGA (*embraces both her sisters*). The music is so gay, so confident, and one longs for life! O my God! Time will pass, and we shall go away for ever, and we shall be forgotten, our faces will be forgotten, our voices, and how many there were of us; but our sufferings will pass into joy for those who will live after us, happiness and peace will be established upon earth, and they will remember kindly and bless those who have lived before. Oh, dear sisters, our life is not ended yet. We shall live! The music is so gay, so joyful, and it seems as though a little more and we shall know what we are living for, why we are suffering.... If we only knew—if we only knew!

(*The music grows more and more subdued;* KULIGIN, *cheerful and smiling, brings the hat and cape;* ANDREY *pushes the perambulator in which* BOBIK *is sitting.*)

TCHEBUTYKIN (*humming softly*). "Tarara-boom-dee-ay!" (*Reads his paper.*) It doesn't matter, it doesn't matter.
OLGA. If we only knew, if we only knew!

CURTAIN.

THE
CHERRY ORCHARD

First performed in Moscow,
January 1904

CHARACTERS IN THE PLAY

MADAME RANEVSKY (LYUBOV ANDREYEVNA) (*the owner of the Cherry Orchard*).
ANYA (*her daughter, aged 17*).
VARYA (*her adopted daughter, aged 24*).
GAEV (LEONID ANDREYEVITCH) (*brother of Madame Ranevsky*).
LOPAHIN (YERMOLAY ALEXEYEVITCH) (*a merchant*).
TROFIMOV (PYOTR SERGEYEVITCH) (*a student*).
SEMYONOV-PISHTCHIK (*a landowner*).
CHARLOTTA IVANOVNA (*a governess*).
EPIHODOV (SEMYON PANTALEYEVITCH) (*a clerk*).
DUNYASHA (*a maid*).
FIRS (*an old valet, aged 87*).
YASHA (*a young valet*).
A VAGRANT.
THE STATION MASTER.
A POST-OFFICE CLERK.
VISITORS, SERVANTS.

The action takes place on the estate of MADAME RANEVSKY.

ACT I

A room, which has always been called the nursery. One of the doors leads into ANYA'S *room. Dawn, sun rises during the scene. May, the cherry trees in flower, but it is cold in the garden with the frost of early morning. Windows closed.*

Enter DUNYASHA *with a candle and* LOPAHIN *with a book in his hand.*

LOPAHIN. The train's in, thank God. What time is it?

DUNYASHA. Nearly two o'clock (*puts out the candle*). It's daylight already.

LOPAHIN. The train's late! Two hours, at least (*yawns and stretches*). I'm a pretty one; what a fool I've been. Came here on purpose to meet them at the station and dropped asleep.... Dozed off as I sat in the chair. It's annoying.... You might have waked me.

DUNYASHA. I thought you had gone (*listens*). There, I do believe they're coming!

LOPAHIN (*listens*). No, what with the luggage and one thing and another (*a pause*). Lyubov Andreyevna has been abroad five years; I don't know what she is like now.... She's a splendid woman. A good-natured, kind-hearted woman. I remember when I was a lad of fifteen, my poor father—he used to keep a little shop here in the village in those days—gave me a punch in the face with his fist and made my nose bleed. We were in the yard here, I forget what we'd come about—he had had a drop. Lyubov Andreyevna—I can see her now—she was a slim young girl then—took me to wash my face, and then brought me into this very room, into the nursery. "Don't cry, little peasant," says she, "it will be well in time for your wedding day" ... (*a pause*). Little peasant.... My father was a peasant, it's true, but here am I in a white waistcoat and brown shoes, like a pig in a bun shop. Yes, I'm a rich man, but for all my money, come to think, a peasant I was, and a peasant I am (*turns over the pages of the book*). I've been reading this book and I can't make head or tail of it. I fell asleep over it (*a pause*).

DUNYASHA. The dogs have been awake all night, they feel that the mistress is coming.

LOPAHIN. Why, what's the matter with you, Dunyasha?

DUNYASHA. My hands are all of a tremble. I feel as though I should faint.

LOPAHIN. You're a spoilt soft creature, Dunyasha. And dressed like a lady too, and your hair done up. That's not the thing. One must know one's place.

(*Enter* EPIHODOV *with a nosegay; he wears a pea-jacket and highly polished creaking topboots; he drops the nosegay as he comes in.*)

EPIHODOV (*picking up the nosegay*). Here! the gardener's sent this, says you're to put it in the dining-room (*gives* DUNYASHA *the nosegay*).

LOPAHIN. And bring me some kvass.

DUNYASHA. I will (*goes out*).

EPIHODOV. It's chilly this morning, three degrees of frost, though the cherries are all in flower. I can't say much for our climate (*sighs*). I can't. Our climate is not often propitious to the occasion. Yermolay Alexeyevitch, permit me to call your attention to the fact that I purchased myself a pair of boots the day before yesterday, and they creak, I venture to assure you, so that there's no tolerating them. What ought I to grease them with?

LOPAHIN. Oh, shut up! Don't bother me.

EPIHODOV. Every day some misfortune befalls me. I don't complain, I'm used to it, and I wear a smiling face.

(DUNYASHA *comes in, hands* LOPAHIN *the kvass.*)

EPIHODOV. I am going (*stumbles against a chair, which falls over*). There! (*As though triumphant*) There you see now, excuse the expression, an accident like that among others.... It's positively remarkable (*goes out*).

DUNYASHA. Do you know, Yermolay Alexeyevitch, I must confess, Epihodov has made me a proposal.

LOPAHIN. Ah!

DUNYASHA. I'm sure I don't know.... He's a harmless fellow, but sometimes when he begins talking, there's no making anything of it. It's all very fine and expressive, only there's no understanding it. I've a sort of liking for him too. He loves me to distraction. He's an unfortunate man; every day there's something. They tease him about it—two and twenty misfortunes they call him.

LOPAHIN (*listening*). There! I do believe they're coming.

DUNYASHA. They are coming! What's the matter with me?... I'm cold all over.

LOPAHIN. They really are coming. Let's go and meet them. Will she know me? It's five years since I saw her.

DUNYASHA (*in a flutter*). I shall drop this very minute.... Ah, I shall drop.

(*There is a sound of two carriages driving up to the house. LOPAHIN and DUN-YASHA go out quickly. The stage is left empty. A noise is heard in the adjoining rooms. FIRS, who has driven to meet MADAME RANEVSKY, crosses the stage hurriedly leaning on a stick. He is wearing old-fashioned livery and a high hat. He says something to himself, but not a word can be distinguished. The noise behind the scenes goes on increasing. A voice: "Come, let's go in here." Enter LYUBOV ANDREYEVNA, ANYA, and CHARLOTTA IVANOVNA with a pet dog on a chain, all in travelling dresses. VARYA in an out-door coat with a kerchief over her head, GAEV, SEMYONOV-PISHTCHIK, LOPAHIN, DUN-YASHA with bag and parasol, servants with other articles. All walk across the room.*)

ANYA. Let's come in here. Do you remember what room this is, mamma?

LYUBOV (*joyfully, through her tears*). The nursery!

VARYA. How cold it is, my hands are numb. (*To* LYUBOV ANDREYEVNA) Your rooms, the white room and the lavender one, are just the same as ever, mamma.

LYUBOV. My nursery, dear delightful room.... I used to sleep here when I was little ... (*cries*). And here I am, like a little child ... (*kisses her brother and* VARYA, *and then her brother again*). Varya's just the same as ever, like a nun. And I knew Dunyasha (*kisses* DUNYASHA).

GAEV. The train was two hours late. What do you think of that? Is that the way to do things?

CHARLOTTA (*to* PISHTCHIK). My dog eats nuts, too.
PISHTCHIK (*wonderingly*). Fancy that!

(*They all go out except* ANYA *and* DUNYASHA.)

DUNYASHA. We've been expecting you so long (*takes* ANYA's *hat and coat*).
ANYA. I haven't slept for four nights on the journey. I feel dreadfully cold.
DUNYASHA. You set out in Lent, there was snow and frost, and now? My darling! (*Laughs and kisses her.*) I *have* missed you, my precious, my joy. I must tell you ... I can't put it off a minute....
ANYA (*wearily*). What now?
DUNYASHA. Epihodov, the clerk, made me a proposal just after Easter.
ANYA. It's always the same thing with you ... (*straightening her hair*). I've lost all my hairpins ... (*she is staggering from exhaustion*).
DUNYASHA. I don't know what to think, really. He does love me, he does love me so!
ANYA (*looking towards her door, tenderly*). My own room, my windows just as though I had never gone away. I'm home! To-morrow morning I shall get up and run into the garden.... Oh, if I could get to sleep! I haven't slept all the journey, I was so anxious and worried.
DUNYASHA. Pyotr Sergeyevitch came the day before yesterday.
ANYA (*joyfully*). Petya!
DUNYASHA. He's asleep in the bath house, he has settled in there. I'm afraid of being in their way, says he. (*Glancing at her watch*) I was to have waked him, but Varvara Mihalovna told me not to. Don't you wake him, says she.

(*Enter* VARYA *with a bunch of keys at her waist.*)

VARYA. Dunyasha, coffee and make haste.... Mamma's asking for coffee.
DUNYASHA. This very minute (*goes out*).
VARYA. Well, thank God, you've come. You're home again (*petting her*).

My little darling has come back! My precious beauty has come back again!

ANYA. I have had a time of it!

VARYA. I can fancy.

ANYA. We set off in Holy Week—it was so cold then, and all the way Charlotta would talk and show off her tricks. What did you want to burden me with Charlotta for?

VARYA. You couldn't have travelled all alone, darling. At seventeen!

ANYA. We got to Paris at last, it was cold there—snow. I speak French shockingly. Mamma lives on the fifth floor, I went up to her and there were a lot of French people, ladies, an old priest with a book. The place smelt of tobacco and so comfortless. I felt sorry, oh! so sorry for mamma all at once, I put my arms round her neck, and hugged her and wouldn't let her go. Mamma was as kind as she could be, and she cried....

VARYA (*through her tears*). Don't speak of it, don't speak of it!

ANYA. She had sold her villa at Mentone, she had nothing left, nothing. I hadn't a farthing left either, we only just had enough to get here. And Mamma doesn't understand! When we had dinner at the stations, she always ordered the most expensive things and gave the waiters a whole rouble. Charlotta's just the same. Yasha too must have the same as we do; it's simply awful. You know Yasha is Mamma's valet now, we brought him here with us.

VARYA. Yes, I've seen the young rascal.

ANYA. Well, tell me—have you paid the arrears on the mortgage?

VARYA. How could we get the money?

ANYA. Oh, dear! Oh, dear!

VARYA. In August the place will be sold.

ANYA. My goodness!

LOPAHIN (*peeps in at the door and moo's like a cow*). Moo! (*Disappears.*)

VARYA (*weeping*). There, that's what I could do to him (*shakes her fist*).

ANYA (*embracing* VARYA, *softly*). Varya, has he made you an offer? (VARYA *shakes her head.*) Why, but he loves you. Why is it you don't come to an understanding? What are you waiting for?

VARYA. I believe that there never will be anything between us. He has a lot to do, he has no time for me ... and takes no notice of me. Bless the man, it makes me miserable to see him.... Everyone's talking of our being married, everyone's congratulating me, and all the while there's really nothing in it; it's all like a dream. (*In another tone*) You have a new brooch like a bee.

ANYA (*mournfully*). Mamma bought it. (*Goes into her own room and in a light-hearted childish tone*) And you know, in Paris I went up in a balloon!

VARYA. My darling's home again! My pretty is home again!

(DUNYASHA *returns with the coffee-pot and is making the coffee.*)

VARYA (*standing at the door*). All day long, darling, as I go about looking after the house, I keep dreaming all the time. If only we could marry you to a rich man, then I should feel more at rest. Then I would go off by myself on a pilgrimage to Kiev, to Moscow ... and so I would spend my life going from one holy place to another.... I would go on and on.... What bliss!

ANYA. The birds are singing in the garden. What time is it?

VARYA. It must be nearly three. It's time you were asleep, darling (*going into* ANYA's *room*). What bliss!

(YASHA *enters with a rug and a travelling bag.*)

YASHA (*crosses the stage, mincingly*). May one come in here, pray?

DUNYASHA. I shouldn't have known you, Yasha. How you have changed abroad.

YASHA. H'm!... And who are you?

DUNYASHA. When you went away, I was that high (*shows distance from floor*). Dunyasha, Fyodor's daughter.... You don't remember me!

YASHA. H'm!... You're a peach! (*Looks round and embraces her: she shrieks and drops a saucer.* YASHA *goes out hastily.*)

VARYA (*in the doorway, in a tone of vexation*). What now?

DUNYASHA (*through her tears*). I have broken a saucer.

VARYA. Well, that brings good luck.

ANYA (*coming out of her room*). We ought to prepare Mamma: Petya is here.

VARYA. I told them not to wake him.

ANYA (*dreamily*). It's six years since father died. Then only a month later little brother Grisha was drowned in the river, such a pretty boy he was, only seven. It was more than Mamma could bear, so she went away, went away without looking back (*shuddering*).... How well I understand her, if only she knew! (*A pause.*) And Petya Trofimov was Grisha's tutor, he may remind her.

(*Enter* FIRS: *he is wearing a pea-jacket and a white waistcoat.*)

FIRS (*goes up to the coffee-pot, anxiously*). The mistress will be served here (*puts on white gloves*). Is the coffee ready? (*Sternly to* DUNYASHA) Girl! Where's the cream?

DUNYASHA. Ah, mercy on us! (*Goes out quickly.*)

FIRS (*fussing round the coffee-pot*). Ech! you good-for-nothing! (*Muttering to himself*) Come back from Paris. And the old master used to go to Paris too ... horses all the way (*laughs*).

VARYA. What is it, Firs?

FIRS. What is your pleasure? (*Gleefully*) My lady has come home! I have lived to see her again! Now I can die (*weeps with joy*).

(*Enter* LYUBOV ANDREYEVNA, GAEV *and* SEMYONOV-PISHTCHIK; *the latter is in a short-waisted full coat of fine cloth, and full trousers.* GAEV, *as he comes in, makes a gesture with his arms and his whole body, as though he were playing billiards.*)

LYUBOV. How does it go? Let me remember. Cannon off the red!

GAEV. That's it—in off the white! Why, once, sister, we used to sleep together in this very room, and now I'm fifty-one, strange as it seems.

LOPAHIN. Yes, time flies.

GAEV. What do you say?

LOPAHIN. Time, I say, flies.

GAEV. What a smell of patchouli!

ANYA. I'm going to bed. Good-night, Mamma (*kisses her mother*).

LYUBOV. My precious darling (*kisses her hands*). Are you glad to be home? I can't believe it.

ANYA. Good-night, Uncle.

GAEV (*kissing her face and hands*). God bless you! How like you are to your mother! (*To his sister*) At her age you were just the same, Lyuba.

(ANYA *shakes hands with* LOPAHIN *and* PISHTCHIK, *then goes out, shutting the door after her.*)

LYUBOV. She's quite worn out.

PISHTCHIK. Aye, it's a long journey, to be sure.

VARYA (*to* LOPAHIN *and* PISHTCHIK). Well, gentlemen? It's three o'clock and time to say good-bye.

LYUBOV (*laughs*). You're just the same as ever, Varya (*draws her to her and kisses her*). I'll just drink my coffee and then we will all go and rest. (FIRS *puts a cushion under her feet.*) Thanks, friend. I am so fond of coffee, I drink it day and night. Thanks, dear old man (*kisses* FIRS).

VARYA. I'll just see whether all the things have been brought in (*goes out*).

LYUBOV. Can it really be me sitting here? (*Laughs.*) I want to dance about and clap my hands. (*Covers her face with her hands*) And I could drop asleep in a moment! God knows I love my country, I love it tenderly; I couldn't look out of the window in the train, I kept crying so. (*Through her tears*) But I must drink my coffee, though. Thank you, Firs, thanks, dear old man. I'm so glad to find you still alive.

FIRS. The day before yesterday.

GAEV. He's rather deaf.

LOPAHIN. I have to set off for Harkov directly, at five o'clock.... It is annoying! I wanted to have a look at you, and a little talk.... You are just as splendid as ever.

PISHTCHIK (*breathing heavily*). Handsomer, indeed.... Dressed in Parisian style ... completely bowled me over.

LOPAHIN. Your brother, Leonid Andreyevitch here, is always saying that I'm a low-born knave, that I'm a money-grubber, but I don't care one straw for that. Let him talk. Only I do want you to believe in me as you used to. I do want your wonderful tender eyes to look at me as they used to in the old days. Merciful God! My father was a serf of your father and of your grandfather, but you—you—did so much for me once, that I've forgotten all that; I love you as though you were my kin ... more than my kin.

LYUBOV. I can't sit still, I simply can't ... (*jumps up and walks about in violent agitation*). This happiness is too much for me.... You may laugh at me, I know I'm silly.... My own bookcase (*kisses the bookcase*). My little table.

GAEV. Nurse died while you were away.

LYUBOV (*sits down and drinks coffee*). Yes, the Kingdom of Heaven be hers! You wrote me of her death.

GAEV. And Anastasy is dead. Squinting Petruchka has left me and is in service now with the police captain in the town (*takes a box of caramels out of his pocket and sucks one*).

PISHTCHIK. My daughter, Dashenka, wishes to be remembered to you.

LOPAHIN. I want to tell you something very pleasant and cheering (*glancing at his watch*). I'm going directly ... there's no time to say much ... well, I can say it in a couple of words. I needn't tell you your cherry orchard is to be sold to pay your debts; the 22nd of August is the date fixed for the sale; but don't you worry, dearest lady, you may sleep in peace, there is a way of saving it.... This is what I propose. I beg your attention! Your estate is not twenty miles from the town, the railway runs close by it, and if the cherry orchard and the land along the river bank were cut up into building plots and then let on lease for summer villas, you would make an income of at least 25,000 roubles a year out of it.

GAEV. That's all rot, if you'll excuse me.

LYUBOV. I don't quite understand you, Yermolay Alexeyevitch.

LOPAHIN. You will get a rent of at least 25 roubles a year for a three-acre plot from summer visitors, and if you say the word now, I'll bet you what you like there won't be one square foot of ground vacant by the autumn, all the plots will be taken up. I congratulate you; in fact, you are saved. It's a perfect situation with that deep river. Only, of course, it must be cleared—all the old buildings, for example, must be removed, this house too, which is really good for nothing, and the old cherry orchard must be cut down.

LYUBOV. Cut down? My dear fellow, forgive me, but you don't know what you are talking about. If there is one thing interesting—remarkable indeed—in the whole province, it's just our cherry orchard.

LOPAHIN. The only thing remarkable about the orchard is that it's a very large one. There's a crop of cherries every alternate year, and then there's nothing to be done with them, no one buys them.

GAEV. This orchard is mentioned in the 'Encyclopædia.'

LOPAHIN (*glancing at his watch*). If we don't decide on something and don't take some steps, on the 22nd of August the cherry orchard and the whole estate too will be sold by auction. Make up your minds! There is no other way of saving it, I'll take my oath on that. No, no!

FIRS. In old days, forty or fifty years ago, they used to dry the cherries, soak them, pickle them, make jam too, and they used——

GAEV. Be quiet, Firs.

FIRS. And they used to send the preserved cherries to Moscow and to Harkov by the waggon-load. That brought the money in! And the preserved cherries in those days were soft and juicy, sweet and fragrant.... They knew the way to do them then....

LYUBOV. And where is the recipe now?

FIRS. It's forgotten. Nobody remembers it.

PISHTCHIK (*to* LYUBOV ANDREYEVNA). What's it like in Paris? Did you eat frogs there?

LYUBOV. Oh, I ate crocodiles.

PISHTCHIK. Fancy that now!

LOPAHIN. There used to be only the gentlefolks and the peasants in the country, but now there are these summer visitors. All the towns, even the small ones, are surrounded nowadays by these summer villas. And one may say for sure, that in another twenty years there'll be many more of these people and that they'll be everywhere. At present the summer visitor only drinks tea in his verandah, but maybe he'll take to working his bit of land too, and then your cherry orchard would become happy, rich and prosperous....

GAEV (*indignant*). What rot!

(*Enter* VARYA *and* YASHA.)

VARYA. There are two telegrams for you, Mamma (*takes out keys and opens an old-fashioned bookcase with a loud crack*). Here they are.

LYUBOV. From Paris (*tears the telegrams, without reading them*). I have done with Paris.

GAEV. Do you know, Lyuba, how old that bookcase is? Last week I pulled out the bottom drawer and there I found the date branded on it. The bookcase was made just a hundred years ago. What do you say to that? We might have celebrated its jubilee. Though it's an inanimate object, still it is a *book* case.

PISHTCHIK (*amazed*). A hundred years! Fancy that now.

GAEV. Yes.... It is a thing ... (*feeling the bookcase*). Dear, honoured, bookcase! Hail to thee who for more than a hundred years hast served the pure ideals of good and justice; thy silent call to fruitful labour has never flagged in those hundred years, maintaining (*in tears*) in the generations of man, courage and faith in a brighter future and fostering in us ideals of good and social consciousness (*a pause*).

LOPAHIN. Yes....

LYUBOV. You are just the same as ever, Leonid.

GAEV (*a little embarrassed*). Cannon off the right into the pocket!

LOPAHIN (*looking at his watch*). Well, it's time I was off.

YASHA (*handing* LYUBOV ANDREYEVNA *medicine*). Perhaps you will take your pills now.

PISHTCHIK. You shouldn't take medicines, my dear madam ... they do no harm and no good. Give them here ... honoured lady (*takes the pill-box, pours the pills into the hollow of his hand, blows on them, puts them in his mouth and drinks off some kvass*). There!

LYUBOV (*in alarm*). Why, you must be out of your mind!

PISHTCHIK. I have taken all the pills.

LOPAHIN. What a glutton! (*All laugh.*)

FIRS. His honour stayed with us in Easter week, ate a gallon and a half of cucumbers ... (*mutters*).

LYUBOV. What is he saying?

VARYA. He has taken to muttering like that for the last three years. We are used to it.

YASHA. His declining years!

(CHARLOTTA IVANOVNA, *a very thin, lanky figure in a white dress with a lorgnette in her belt, walks across the stage.*)

LOPAHIN. I beg your pardon, Charlotta Ivanovna, I have not had time to greet you (*tries to kiss her hand*).

CHARLOTTA (*pulling away her hand*). If I let you kiss my hand, you'll be wanting to kiss my elbow, and then my shoulder.

LOPAHIN. I've no luck to-day! (*All laugh.*) Charlotta Ivanovna, show us some tricks!

LYUBOV. Charlotta, do show us some tricks!

CHARLOTTA. I don't want to. I'm sleepy (*goes out*).

LOPAHIN. In three weeks' time we shall meet again (*kisses LYUBOV ANDREYEVNA's hand*). Good-bye till then—I must go. (*To GAEV*) Good-bye. (*Kisses PISHTCHIK*) Good-bye. (*Gives his hand to VARYA, then to FIRS and YASHA*) I don't want to go. (*To LYUBOV ANDREYEVNA*) If you think over my plan for the villas and make up your mind, then let me know; I will lend you 50,000 roubles. Think of it seriously.

VARYA (*angrily*). Well, do go, for goodness sake.

LOPAHIN. I'm going, I'm going (*goes out*).

GAEV. Low-born knave! I beg pardon, though ... Varya is going to marry him, he's Varya's fiancé.

VARYA. Don't talk nonsense, uncle.

LYUBOV. Well, Varya, I shall be delighted. He's a good man.

PISHTCHIK. He is, one must acknowledge, a most worthy man. And my Dashenka ... says too that ... she says ... various things (*snores, but at once wakes up*). But all the same, honoured lady, could you oblige me ... with a loan of 240 roubles ... to pay the interest on my mortgage to-morrow?

VARYA (*dismayed*). No, no.

LYUBOV. I really haven't any money.

PISHTCHIK. It will turn up (*laughs*). I never lose hope. I thought everything was over, I was a ruined man, and lo and behold—the railway passed through my land and ... they paid me for it. And something else will turn up again, if not to-day, then to-morrow ... Dashenka'll win two hundred thousand ... she's got a lottery ticket.

LYUBOV. Well, we've finished our coffee, we can go to bed.

FIRS (*brushes* GAEV, *reprovingly*). You have got on the wrong trousers again! What am I to do with you?

VARYA (*softly*). Anya's asleep. (*Softly opens the window*) Now the sun's risen, it's not a bit cold. Look, mamma, what exquisite trees! My goodness! And the air! The starlings are singing!

GAEV (*opens another window*). The orchard is all white. You've not forgotten it, Lyuba? That long avenue that runs straight, straight as an arrow, how it shines on a moonlight night. You remember? You've not forgotten?

LYUBOV (*looking out of the window into the garden*). Oh, my childhood, my innocence! It was in this nursery I used to sleep, from here I looked out into the orchard, happiness waked with me every morning and in those days the orchard was just the same, nothing has changed (*laughs with delight*). All, all white! Oh, my orchard! After the dark gloomy autumn, and the cold winter; you are young again, and full of happiness, the heavenly angels have never left you.... If I could cast off the burden that weighs on my heart, if I could forget the past!

GAEV. H'm! and the orchard will be sold to pay our debts; it seems strange....

LYUBOV. See, our mother walking ... all in white, down the avenue! (*Laughs with delight.*) It is she!

GAEV. Where?

VARYA. Oh, don't, Mamma!

LYUBOV. There is no one. It was my fancy. On the right there, by the path to the arbour, there is a white tree bending like a woman....

(*Enter* TROFIMOV *wearing a shabby student's uniform and spectacles.*)

LYUBOV. What a ravishing orchard! White masses of blossom, blue sky....

TROFIMOV. Lyubov Andreyevna! (*She looks round at him.*) I will just pay my respects to you and then leave you at once (*kisses her hand warmly*). I was told to wait until morning, but I hadn't the patience to wait any longer....

(Lyubov Andreyevna *looks at him in perplexity.*)

Varya (*through her tears*). This is Petya Trofimov.

Trofimov. Petya Trofimov, who was your Grisha's tutor.... Can I have changed so much?

(Lyubov Andreyevna *embraces him and weeps quietly.*)

Gaev (*in confusion*). There, there, Lyuba.

Varya (*crying*). I told you, Petya, to wait till to-morrow.

Lyubov. My Grisha ... my boy ... Grisha ... my son!

Varya. We can't help it, Mamma, it is God's will.

Trofimov (*softly through his tears*). There ... there.

Lyubov (*weeping quietly*). My boy was lost ... drowned. Why? Oh, why, dear Petya? (*More quietly*) Anya is asleep in there, and I'm talking loudly ... making this noise.... But, Petya? Why have you grown so ugly? Why do you look so old?

Trofimov. A peasant-woman in the train called me a mangy-looking gentleman.

Lyubov. You were quite a boy then, a pretty little student, and now your hair's thin—and spectacles. Are you really a student still? (*Goes towards the door.*)

Trofimov. I seem likely to be a perpetual student.

Lyubov (*kisses her brother, then* Varya). Well, go to bed.... You are older too, Leonid.

Pishtchik (*follows her*). I suppose it's time we were asleep.... Ugh! my gout. I'm staying the night! Lyubov Andreyevna, my dear soul, if you could ... to-morrow morning ... 240 roubles.

Gaev. That's always his story.

Pishtchik. 240 roubles ... to pay the interest on my mortgage.

Lyubov. My dear man, I have no money.

Pishtchik. I'll pay it back, my dear ... a trifling sum.

Lyubov. Oh, well, Leonid will give it you.... You give him the money, Leonid.

Gaev. Me give it him! Let him wait till he gets it!

Lyubov. It can't be helped, give it him. He needs it. He'll pay it back.

(LYUBOV ANDREYEVNA, TROFIMOV, PISHTCHIK *and* FIRS *go out.* GAEV, VARYA *and* YASHA *remain.*)

GAEV. Sister hasn't got out of the habit of flinging away her money. (*To* YASHA) Get away, my good fellow, you smell of the hen-house.

YASHA (*with a grin*). And you, Leonid Andreyevitch, are just the same as ever.

GAEV. What's that? (*To* VARYA) What did he say?

VARYA (*to* YASHA). Your mother has come from the village; she has been sitting in the servants' room since yesterday, waiting to see you.

YASHA. Oh, bother her!

VARYA. For shame!

YASHA. What's the hurry? She might just as well have come to-morrow (*goes out*).

VARYA. Mamma's just the same as ever, she hasn't changed a bit. If she had her own way, she'd give away everything.

GAEV. Yes (*a pause*). If a great many remedies are suggested for some disease, it means that the disease is incurable. I keep thinking and racking my brains; I have many schemes, a great many, and that really means none. If we could only come in for a legacy from somebody, or marry our Anya to a very rich man, or we might go to Yaroslavl and try our luck with our old aunt, the Countess. She's very, very rich, you know.

VARYA (*weeps*). If God would help us.

GAEV. Don't blubber. Aunt's very rich, but she doesn't like us. First, sister married a lawyer instead of a nobleman....

(ANYA *appears in the doorway.*)

GAEV. And then her conduct, one can't call it virtuous. She is good, and kind, and nice, and I love her, but, however one allows for ex-tenuating circumstances, there's no denying that she's an immoral woman. One feels it in her slightest gesture.

VARYA (*in a whisper*). Anya's in the doorway.

GAEV. What do you say? (*A pause.*) It's queer, there seems to be some-thing wrong with my right eye. I don't see as well as I did. And on Thursday when I was in the district Court ...

(*Enter* ANYA.)

VARYA. Why aren't you asleep, Anya?

ANYA. I can't get to sleep.

GAEV. My pet (*kisses* ANYA's *face and hands*). My child (*weeps*). You are not my niece, you are my angel, you are everything to me. Believe me, believe ...

ANYA. I believe you, Uncle. Everyone loves you and respects you ... but, Uncle dear, you must be silent ... simply be silent. What were you saying just now about my mother, about your own sister? What made you say that?

GAEV. Yes, yes ... (*puts his hand over his face*). Really, that was awful! My God, save me! And to-day I made a speech to the book-case ... so stupid! And only when I had finished, I saw how stupid it was.

VARYA. It's true, Uncle, you ought to keep quiet. Don't talk, that's all.

ANYA. If you could keep from talking, it would make things easier for you, too.

GAEV. I won't speak (*kisses* ANYA's *and* VARYA's *hands*). I'll be silent. Only this is about business. On Thursday I was in the district Court; well, there was a large party of us there and we began talking of one thing and another, and this and that, and do you know, I believe that it will be possible to raise a loan on an I.O.U. to pay the arrears on the mortgage.

VARYA. If the Lord would help us!

GAEV. I'm going on Tuesday; I'll talk of it again. (*To* VARYA) Don't blubber. (*To* ANYA) Your mamma will talk to Lopahin; of course, he won't refuse her. And as soon as you're rested you shall go to Yaroslavl to the Countess, your great-aunt. So we shall all set to work in three directions at once, and the business is done. We shall pay off arrears, I'm convinced of it (*puts a caramel in his mouth*). I swear on my honour, I swear by anything you like, the estate shan't be sold. (*Excitedly*) By my own happiness, I swear it! Here's my hand on it, call me the basest, vilest of men, if I let it come to an auction! Upon my soul I swear it!

ANYA (*her equanimity has returned, she is quite happy*). How good you are,

Uncle, and how clever! (*Embraces her uncle.*) I'm at peace now! Quite at peace! I'm happy!

(*Enter* FIRS.)

FIRS (*reproachfully*). Leonid Andreyevitch, have you no fear of God? When are you going to bed?

GAEV. Directly, directly. You can go, Firs. I'll ... yes, I will undress myself. Come, children, bye-bye. We'll go into details to-morrow, but now go to bed (*kisses* ANYA *and* VARYA). I'm a man of the eighties. They run down that period, but still I can say I have had to suffer not a little for my convictions in my life. It's not for nothing that the peasant loves me. One must know the peasant! One must know how ...

ANYA. At it again, Uncle!

VARYA. Uncle dear, you'd better be quiet!

FIRS (*angrily*). Leonid Andreyevitch!

GAEV. I'm coming. I'm coming. Go to bed. Potted the shot—there's a shot for you! A beauty! (*Goes out,* FIRS *hobbling after him.*)

ANYA. My mind's at rest now. I don't want to go to Yaroslavl, I don't like my great-aunt, but still my mind's at rest. Thanks to Uncle (*sits down*).

VARYA. We must go to bed. I'm going. Something unpleasant happened while you were away. In the old servants' quarters there are only the old servants, as you know—Efimyushka, Polya and Yevstigney—and Karp too. They began letting stray people in to spend the night—I said nothing. But all at once I heard they had been spreading a report that I gave them nothing but pease pudding to eat. Out of stinginess, you know.... And it was all Yevstigney's doing.... Very well, I said to myself.... If that's how it is, I thought, wait a bit. I sent for Yevstigney ... (*yawns*). He comes.... "How's this, Yevstigney," I said, "you could be such a fool as to?..." (*Looking at* ANYA) Anitchka! (*A pause.*) She's asleep (*puts her arm round* ANYA). Come to bed ... come along! (*Leads her.*) My darling has fallen asleep! Come ... (*They go.*)

(*Far away beyond the orchard a shepherd plays on a pipe.* TROFIMOV *crosses the stage and, seeing* VARYA *and* ANYA, *stands still.*)

VARYA. 'Sh! asleep, asleep. Come, my own.

ANYA (*softly, half asleep*). I'm so tired. Still those bells. Uncle ... dear ... Mamma and Uncle....

VARYA. Come, my own, come along.

(*They go into* ANYA'S *room.*)

TROFIMOV (*tenderly*). My sunshine! My spring.

CURTAIN.

ACT II

The open country. An old shrine, long abandoned and fallen out of the perpendicular; near it a well, large stones that have apparently once been tombstones, and an old garden seat. The road to GAEV'S *house is seen. On one side rise dark poplars; and there the cherry orchard begins. In the distance a row of telegraph poles and far, far away on the horizon there is faintly outlined a great town, only visible in very fine clear weather. It is near sunset.* CHARLOTTA, YASHA *and* DUNYASHA *are sitting on the seat.* EPIHODOV *is standing near, playing something mournful on a guitar. All sit plunged in thought.* CHARLOTTA *wears an old forage cap; she has taken a gun from her shoulder and is tightening the buckle on the strap.*

CHARLOTTA (*musingly*). I haven't a real passport of my own, and I don't know how old I am, and I always feel that I'm a young thing. When I was a little girl, my father and mother used to travel about to fairs and give performances—very good ones. And I used to dance *salto-mortale* and all sorts of things. And when Papa and Mamma died, a German lady took me and had me educated. And so I grew up and became a governess. But where I came from, and who I am, I don't know.... Who my parents were, very likely they weren't married ... I don't know (*takes a cucumber out of her pocket and eats*). I know nothing at all (*a pause*). One wants to talk and has no one to talk to ... I have nobody.

EPIHODOV (*plays on the guitar and sings*). "What care I for the noisy world! What care I for friends or foes!" How agreeable it is to play on the mandoline!

DUNYASHA. That's a guitar, not a mandoline (*looks in a hand-mirror and powders herself*).

EPIHODOV. To a man mad with love, it's a mandoline. (*Sings*) "Were her heart but aglow with love's mutual flame." (YASHA *joins in.*)

CHARLOTTA. How shockingly these people sing! Foo! Like jackals!

DUNYASHA (*to* YASHA). What happiness, though, to visit foreign lands.

YASHA. Ah, yes! I rather agree with you there (*yawns, then lights a cigar*).

EPIHODOV. That's comprehensible. In foreign lands everything has long since reached full complexion.

YASHA. That's so, of course.

EPIHODOV. I'm a cultivated man, I read remarkable books of all sorts, but I can never make out the tendency I am myself precisely inclined for, whether to live or to shoot myself, speaking precisely, but nevertheless I always carry a revolver. Here it is ... (*shows revolver*).

CHARLOTTA. I've had enough, and now I'm going (*puts on the gun*). Epihodov, you're a very clever fellow, and a very terrible one too, all the women must be wild about you. Br-r-r! (*Goes.*) These clever fellows are all so stupid; there's not a creature for me to speak to.... Always alone, alone, nobody belonging to me ... and who I am, and why I'm on earth, I don't know (*walks away slowly*).

EPIHODOV. Speaking precisely, not touching upon other subjects, I'm bound to admit about myself that destiny behaves mercilessly to me, as a storm to a little boat. If, let us suppose, I am mistaken, then why did I wake up this morning, to quote an example, and look round, and there on my chest was a spider of fearful magnitude ... like this (*shows with both hands*). And then I take up a jug of kvass, to quench my thirst, and in it there is something in the highest degree unseemly of the nature of a cockroach (*a pause*). Have you read Buckle? (*A pause.*) I am desirous of troubling you, Dunyasha, with a couple of words.

DUNYASHA. Well, speak.

EPIHODOV. I should be desirous to speak with you alone (*sighs*).

DUNYASHA (*embarrassed*). Well—only bring me my mantle first. It's by the cupboard. It's rather damp here.

EPIHODOV. Certainly. I will fetch it. Now I know what I must do with my revolver (*takes guitar and goes off playing on it*).

YASHA. Two and twenty misfortunes! Between ourselves, he's a fool (*yawns*).

DUNYASHA. God grant he doesn't shoot himself! (*A pause.*) I am so nervous, I'm always in a flutter. I was a little girl when I was taken into our lady's house, and now I have quite grown out of peasant ways, and my hands are white, as white as a lady's. I'm such a delicate, sensitive creature, I'm afraid of everything. I'm so frightened. And if you deceive me, Yasha, I don't know what will become of my nerves.

YASHA (*kisses her*). You're a peach! Of course a girl must never forget herself; what I dislike more than anything is a girl being flighty in her behaviour.

DUNYASHA. I'm passionately in love with you, Yasha; you are a man of culture—you can give your opinion about anything (*a pause*).

YASHA (*yawns*). Yes, that's so. My opinion is this: if a girl loves anyone, that means that she has no principles (*a pause*). It's pleasant smoking a cigar in the open air (*listens*). Someone's coming this way ... it's the gentlefolk (DUNYASHA *embraces him impulsively*). Go home, as though you had been to the river to bathe; go by that path, or else they'll meet you and suppose I have made an appointment with you here. That I can't endure.

DUNYASHA (*coughing softly*). The cigar has made my head ache ... (*goes off*).

(YASHA *remains sitting near the shrine. Enter* LYUBOV ANDREYEVNA, GAEV *and* LOPAHIN.)

LOPAHIN. You must make up your mind once for all—there's no time to lose. It's quite a simple question, you know. Will you consent to letting the land for building or not? One word in answer: Yes or no? Only one word!

LYUBOV. Who is smoking such horrible cigars here? (*Sits down.*)

GAEV. Now the railway line has been brought near, it's made things very convenient (*sits down*). Here we have been over and lunched in town. Cannon off the white! I should like to go home and have a game.

LYUBOV. You have plenty of time.

LOPAHIN. Only one word! (*Beseechingly*) Give me an answer!

GAEV (*yawning*). What do you say?

LYUBOV (*looks in her purse*). I had quite a lot of money here yesterday, and there's scarcely any left to-day. My poor Varya feeds us all on milk soup for the sake of economy; the old folks in the kitchen get nothing but pease pudding, while I waste my money in a senseless way (*drops purse, scattering gold pieces*). There, they have all fallen out! (*annoyed*)

YASHA. Allow me, I'll soon pick them up (*collects the coins*).

LYUBOV. Pray do, Yasha. And what did I go off to the town to lunch for? Your restaurant's a wretched place with its music and the tablecloth smelling of soap.... Why drink so much, Leonid? And eat so much? And talk so much? To-day you talked a great deal again in the restaurant, and all so inappropriately. About the era of the 'seventies, about the decadents. And to whom? Talking to waiters about decadents!

LOPAHIN. Yes.

GAEV (*waving his hand*). I'm incorrigible; that's evident. (*Irritably to* YASHA) Why is it you keep fidgeting about in front of us!

YASHA (*laughs*). I can't help laughing when I hear your voice.

GAEV (*to his sister*). Either I or he ...

LYUBOV. Get along! Go away, Yasha.

YASHA (*gives* LYUBOV ANDREYEVNA *her purse*). Directly (*hardly able to suppress his laughter*). This minute ... (*goes off*).

LOPAHIN. Deriganov, the millionaire, means to buy your estate. They say he is coming to the sale himself.

LYUBOV. Where did you hear that?

LOPAHIN. That's what they say in town.

GAEV. Our aunt in Yaroslavl has promised to send help; but when, and how much she will send, we don't know.

LOPAHIN. How much will she send? A hundred thousand? Two hundred?

LYUBOV. Oh, well!... Ten or fifteen thousand, and we must be thankful to get that.

LOPAHIN. Forgive me, but such reckless people as you are—such queer, unbusiness-like people—I never met in my life. One tells you in plain Russian your estate is going to be sold, and you seem not to understand it.

LYUBOV. What are we to do? Tell us what to do.

LOPAHIN. I do tell you every day. Every day I say the same thing. You absolutely must let the cherry orchard and the land on building leases; and do it at once, as quick as may be—the auction's close upon us! Do understand! Once make up your mind to build villas, and you can raise as much money as you like, and then you are saved.

LYUBOV. Villas and summer visitors—forgive me saying so—it's so vulgar.

GAEV. There I perfectly agree with you.

LOPAHIN. I shall sob, or scream, or fall into a fit. I can't stand it! You drive me mad! (*To* GAEV) You're an old woman!

GAEV. What do you say?

LOPAHIN. An old woman! (*Gets up to go.*)

LYUBOV (*in dismay*). No, don't go! Do stay, my dear friend! Perhaps we shall think of something.

LOPAHIN. What is there to think of?

LYUBOV. Don't go, I entreat you! With you here it's more cheerful, any-way (*a pause*). I keep expecting something, as though the house were going to fall about our ears.

GAEV (*in profound dejection*). Potted the white! It fails—a kiss.

LYUBOV. We have been great sinners....

LOPAHIN. You have no sins to repent of.

GAEV (*puts a caramel in his mouth*). They say I've eaten up my property in caramels (*laughs*).

LYUBOV. Oh, my sins! I've always thrown my money away reck-lessly like a lunatic. I married a man who made nothing but debts. My husband died of champagne—he drank dreadfully. To my misery I loved another man, and immediately—it was my first punishment—the blow fell upon me, here, in the river ... my boy was drowned and I went abroad—went away for ever, never to re-turn, not to see that river again ... I shut my eyes, and fled, dis-tracted, and *he* after me ... pitilessly, brutally. I bought a villa at Mentone, for *he* fell ill there, and for three years I had no rest day or night. His illness wore me out, my soul was dried up. And last year, when my villa was sold to pay my debts, I went to Paris and there he robbed me of everything and abandoned me for another woman; and I tried to poison myself.... So stupid, so shameful!... And suddenly I felt a yearning for Russia, for my country, for my little girl ... (*dries her tears*). Lord, Lord, be merciful! Forgive my sins! Do not chastise me more! (*Takes a telegram out of her pocket*) I got this to-day from Paris. He implores forgiveness, entreats me to return (*tears up the telegram*). I fancy there is music somewhere (*listens*).

GAEV. That's our famous Jewish orchestra. You remember, four violins, a flute and a double bass.

LYUBOV. That still in existence? We ought to send for them one evening, and give a dance.

LOPAHIN (*listens*). I can't hear.... (*Hums softly*) "For money the Germans will turn a Russian into a Frenchman." (*Laughs*) I did see such a piece at the theatre yesterday! It was funny!

LYUBOV. And most likely there was nothing funny in it. You shouldn't look at plays, you should look at yourselves a little oftener. How grey your lives are! How much nonsense you talk.

LOPAHIN. That's true. One may say honestly, we live a fool's life (*pause*). My father was a peasant, an idiot; he knew nothing and taught me nothing, only beat me when he was drunk, and always with his stick. In reality I am just such another blockhead and idiot. I've learnt nothing properly. I write a wretched hand. I write so that I feel ashamed before folks, like a pig.

LYUBOV. You ought to get married, my dear fellow.

LOPAHIN. Yes ... that's true.

LYUBOV. You should marry our Varya, she's a good girl.

LOPAHIN. Yes.

LYUBOV. She's a good-natured girl, she's busy all day long, and what's more, she loves you. And you have liked her for ever so long.

LOPAHIN. Well? I'm not against it.... She's a good girl (*pause*).

GAEV. I've been offered a place in the bank: 6,000 roubles a year. Did you know?

LYUBOV. You would never do for that! You must stay as you are.

(*Enter* FIRS *with overcoat.*)

FIRS. Put it on, sir, it's damp.

GAEV (*putting it on*). You bother me, old fellow.

FIRS. You can't go on like this. You went away in the morning without leaving word (*looks him over*).

LYUBOV. You look older, Firs!

FIRS. What is your pleasure?

LOPAHIN. You look older, she said.

FIRS. I've had a long life. They were arranging my wedding before your papa was born … (*laughs*). I was the head footman before the emancipation came. I wouldn't consent to be set free then; I stayed on with the old master … (*a pause*). I remember what rejoicings they made and didn't know themselves what they were rejoicing over.

LOPAHIN. Those were fine old times. There was flogging anyway.

FIRS (*not hearing*). To be sure! The peasants knew their place, and the masters knew theirs; but now they're all at sixes and sevens, there's no making it out.

GAEV. Hold your tongue, Firs. I must go to town to-morrow. I have been promised an introduction to a general, who might let us have a loan.

LOPAHIN. You won't bring that off. And you won't pay your arrears, you may rest assured of that.

LYUBOV. That's all his nonsense. There is no such general.

(*Enter* TROFIMOV, ANYA *and* VARYA.)

GAEV. Here come our girls.

ANYA. There's Mamma on the seat.

LYUBOV (*tenderly*). Come here, come along. My darlings! (*Embraces* ANYA *and* VARYA.) If you only knew how I love you both. Sit beside me, there, like that. (*All sit down.*)

LOPAHIN. Our perpetual student is always with the young ladies.

TROFIMOV. That's not your business.

LOPAHIN. He'll soon be fifty, and he's still a student.

TROFIMOV. Drop your idiotic jokes.

LOPAHIN. Why are you so cross, you queer fish?

TROFIMOV. Oh, don't persist!

LOPAHIN (*laughs*). Allow me to ask you what's your idea of me?

TROFIMOV. I'll tell you my idea of you, Yermolay Alexeyevitch: you are a rich man, you'll soon be a millionaire. Well, just as in the economy of nature a wild beast is of use, who devours everything that comes in his way, so you too have your use.

(*All laugh.*)

VARYA. Better tell us something about the planets, Petya.

LYUBOV. No, let us go on with the conversation we had yesterday.

TROFIMOV. What was it about?

GAEV. About pride.

TROFIMOV. We had a long conversation yesterday, but we came to no conclusion. In pride, in your sense of it, there is something mystical. Perhaps you are right from your point of view; but if one looks at it simply, without subtlety, what sort of pride can there be, what sense is there in it, if man in his physiological formation is very imperfect, if in the immense majority of cases he is coarse, dull-witted, profoundly unhappy? One must give up glorification of self. One should work, and nothing else.

GAEV. One must die in any case.

TROFIMOV. Who knows? And what does it mean—dying? Perhaps man has a hundred senses, and only the five we know are lost at death, while the other ninety-five remain alive.

LYUBOV. How clever you are, Petya!

LOPAHIN (*ironically*). Fearfully clever!

TROFIMOV. Humanity progresses, perfecting its powers. Everything that is beyond its ken now will one day become familiar and comprehensible; only we must work, we must with all our powers aid the seeker after truth. Here among us in Russia the workers are few in number as yet. The vast majority of the intellectual people I know seek nothing, do nothing, are not fit as yet for work of any kind. They call themselves intellectual, but they treat their servants as inferiors, behave to the peasants as though they were animals, learn little, read nothing seriously, do practically nothing, only talk about science and know very little about art. They are all serious people, they all have severe faces, they all talk of weighty matters and air their theories, and yet the vast majority of us—ninety-nine per cent.—live like savages, at the least thing fly to blows and abuse, eat piggishly, sleep in filth and stuffiness, bugs everywhere, stench and damp and moral impurity. And it's clear all our fine talk is only to divert our attention and other people's. Show me where to find the crèches there's so much talk about, and the reading-rooms? They only exist in novels: in real life there are none of them. There is nothing but filth and vulgarity and Asiatic apathy. I fear and dislike very serious faces. I'm afraid of serious conversations. We should do better to be silent.

LOPAHIN. You know, I get up at five o'clock in the morning, and I work from morning to night; and I've money, my own and other people's, always passing through my hands, and I see what people are made of all round me. One has only to begin to do anything to see how few honest, decent people there are. Sometimes when I lie awake at night, I think: "Oh! Lord, thou hast given us immense forests, boundless plains, the widest horizons, and living here we ourselves ought really to be giants."

LYUBOV. You ask for giants! They are no good except in story-books; in real life they frighten us.

(EPIHODOV *advances in the background, playing on the guitar.*)

LYUBOV (*dreamily*). There goes Epihodov.
ANYA (*dreamily*). There goes Epihodov.
GAEV. The sun has set, my friends.
TROFIMOV. Yes.
GAEV (*not loudly, but, as it were, declaiming*). O nature, divine nature, thou art bright with eternal lustre, beautiful and indifferent! Thou, whom we call mother, thou dost unite within thee life and death! Thou dost give life and dost destroy!
VARYA (*in a tone of supplication*). Uncle!
ANYA. Uncle, you are at it again!
TROFIMOV. You'd much better be cannoning off the red!
GAEV. I'll hold my tongue, I will.

(*All sit plunged in thought. Perfect stillness. The only thing audible is the muttering of* FIRS. *Suddenly there is a sound in the distance, as it were from the sky—the sound of a breaking harp-string, mournfully dying away.*)

LYUBOV. What is that?
LOPAHIN. I don't know. Somewhere far away a bucket fallen and broken in the pits. But somewhere very far away.

GAEV. It might be a bird of some sort—such as a heron.

TROFIMOV. Or an owl.

LYUBOV (*shudders*). I don't know why, but it's horrid (*a pause*).

FIRS. It was the same before the calamity—the owl hooted and the samovar hissed all the time.

GAEV. Before what calamity?

FIRS. Before the emancipation (*a pause*).

LYUBOV. Come, my friends, let us be going; evening is falling. (*To* ANYA) There are tears in your eyes. What is it, darling? (*Embraces her.*)

ANYA. Nothing, Mamma; it's nothing.

TROFIMOV. There is somebody coming.

(*The wayfarer appears in a shabby white forage cap and an overcoat; he is slightly drunk.*)

WAYFARER. Allow me to inquire, can I get to the station this way?

GAEV. Yes. Go along that road.

WAYFARER. I thank you most feelingly (*coughing*). The weather is superb. (*Declaims*) My brother, my suffering brother! ... Come out to the Volga! Whose groan do you hear? ... (*To* VARYA) Mademoiselle, vouchsafe a hungry Russian thirty kopeks.

(VARYA *utters a shriek of alarm.*)

LOPAHIN (*angrily*). There's a right and a wrong way of doing everything!

LYUBOV (*hurriedly*). Here, take this (*looks in her purse*). I've no silver. No matter—here's gold for you.

WAYFARER. I thank you most feelingly! (*Goes off.*)

(*Laughter.*)

VARYA (*frightened*). I'm going home—I'm going ... Oh, Mamma, the servants have nothing to eat, and you gave him gold!

LYUBOV. There's no doing anything with me. I'm so silly! When we get

home, I'll give you all I possess. Yermolay Alexeyevitch, you will
lend me some more ...!

LOPAHIN. I will.

LYUBOV. Come, friends, it's time to be going. And Varya, we have made
a match of it for you. I congratulate you.

VARYA (*through her tears*). Mamma, that's not a joking matter.

LOPAHIN. "Ophelia, get thee to a nunnery!"

GAEV. My hands are trembling; it's a long while since I had a game of
billiards.

LOPAHIN. "Ophelia! Nymph, in thy orisons be all my sins remember'd."

LYUBOV. Come, it will soon be supper-time.

VARYA. How he frightened me! My heart's simply throbbing.

LOPAHIN. Let me remind you, ladies and gentlemen: on the 22nd of
August the cherry orchard will be sold. Think about that! Think
about it!

(*All go off, except* TROFIMOV *and* ANYA.)

ANYA (*laughing*). I'm grateful to the wayfarer! He frightened Varya and
we are left alone.

TROFIMOV. Varya's afraid we shall fall in love with each other, and for
days together she won't leave us. With her narrow brain she can't
grasp that we are above love. To eliminate the petty and transitory
which hinders us from being free and happy—that is the aim and
meaning of our life. Forward! We go forward irresistibly towards
the bright star that shines yonder in the distance. Forward! Do not
lag behind, friends.

ANYA (*claps her hands*). How well you speak! (*A pause.*) It is divine here
to-day.

TROFIMOV. Yes, it's glorious weather.

ANYA. Somehow, Petya, you've made me so that I don't love the cherry
orchard as I used to. I used to love it so dearly. I used to think that
there was no spot on earth like our garden.

TROFIMOV. All Russia is our garden. The earth is great and beautiful—
there are many beautiful places in it (*a pause*). Think only, Anya,
your grandfather, and great-grandfather, and all your ancestors

were slave-owners—the owners of living souls—and from every cherry in the orchard, from every leaf, from every trunk there are human creatures looking at you. Cannot you hear their voices? Oh, it is awful! Your orchard is a fearful thing, and when in the evening or at night one walks about the orchard, the old bark on the trees glimmers dimly in the dusk, and the old cherry trees seem to be dreaming of centuries gone by and tortured by fearful visions. Yes! We are at least two hundred years behind, we have really gained nothing yet, we have no definite attitude to the past, we do nothing but theorise or complain of depression or drink vodka. It is clear that to begin to live in the present we must first expiate our past, we must break with it; and we can expiate it only by suffering, by extraordinary unceasing labour. Understand that, Anya.

ANYA. The house we live in has long ceased to be our own, and I shall leave it, I give you my word.

TROFIMOV. If you have the house keys, fling them into the well and go away. Be free as the wind.

ANYA (*in ecstasy*). How beautifully you said that!

TROFIMOV. Believe me, Anya, believe me! I am not thirty yet, I am young, I am still a student, but I have gone through so much already! As soon as winter comes I am hungry, sick, careworn, poor as a beggar, and what ups and downs of fortune have I not known! And my soul was always, every minute, day and night, full of inexplicable forebodings. I have a foreboding of happiness, Anya. I see glimpses of it already.

ANYA (*pensively*). The moon is rising.

(EPIHODOV *is heard playing still the same mournful song on the guitar. The moon rises. Somewhere near the poplars* VARYA *is looking for* ANYA *and calling* "Anya! where are you?")

TROFIMOV. Yes, the moon is rising (*a pause*). Here is happiness—here it comes! It is coming nearer and nearer; already I can hear its footsteps. And if we never see it—if we may never know it—what does it matter? Others will see it after us.

VARYA'S VOICE. Anya! Where are you?

TROFIMOV. That Varya again! (*Angrily*) It's revolting!
ANYA. Well, let's go down to the river. It's lovely there.
TROFIMOV. Yes, let's go. (*They go.*)
VARYA'S VOICE. Anya! Anya!

CURTAIN.

ACT III

A drawing-room divided by an arch from a larger drawing-room. A chandelier burning. The Jewish orchestra, the same that was mentioned in Act II, is heard playing in the ante-room. It is evening. In the larger drawing-room they are dancing the grand chain. The voice of Semyonov-Pishtchik: *"Promenade à une paire!" Then enter the drawing-room in couples first* Pishtchik *and* Charlotta Ivanova, *then* Trofimov *and* Lyubov Andreyevna, *thirdly* Anya *with the Post-Office Clerk, fourthly* Varya *with the Station Master, and other guests.* Varya *is quietly weeping and wiping away her tears as she dances. In the last couple is* Dunyasha. *They move across the drawing-room.* Pishtchik *shouts:* "Grand rond, balancez!" *and* "Les Cavaliers à genou et remerciez vos dames."

Firs in a swallow-tail coat brings in seltzer water on a tray. Pishtchik *and* Trofimov *enter the drawing-room.*

Pishtchik. I am a full-blooded man; I have already had two strokes. Dancing's hard work for me, but as they say, if you're in the pack, you must bark with the rest. I'm as strong, I may say, as a horse. My parent, who would have his joke—may the Kingdom of Heaven be his!—used to say about our origin that the ancient stock of the Semyonov-Pishtchiks was derived from the very horse that Caligula made a member of the senate (*sits down*). But I've no money, that's where the mischief is. A hungry dog believes in nothing but meat ... (*snores, but at once wakes up*). That's like me ... I can think of nothing but money.

Trofimov. There really is something horsy about your appearance.

Pishtchik. Well ... a horse is a fine beast ... a horse can be sold.

(*There is the sound of billiards being played in an adjoining room.* Varya *appears in the arch leading to the larger drawing-room.*)

TROFIMOV (*teasing*). Madame Lopahin! Madame Lopahin!

VARYA (*angrily*). Mangy-looking gentleman!

TROFIMOV. Yes, I am a mangy-looking gentleman, and I'm proud of it!

VARYA (*pondering bitterly*). Here we have hired musicians and nothing to pay them! (*Goes out.*)

TROFIMOV (*to* PISHTCHIK). If the energy you have wasted during your lifetime in trying to find the money to pay your interest had gone to something else, you might in the end have turned the world upside down.

PISHTCHIK. Nietzsche, the philosopher, a very great and celebrated man … of enormous intellect … says in his works, that one can make forged bank-notes.

TROFIMOV. Why, have you read Nietzsche?

PISHTCHIK. What next … Dashenka told me…. And now I am in such a position, I might just as well forge bank-notes. The day after tomorrow I must pay 310 roubles—130 I have procured (*feels in his pockets, in alarm*). The money's gone! I have lost my money! (*Through his tears*) Where's the money? (*Gleefully*) Why, here it is behind the lining…. It has made me hot all over.

(*Enter* LYUBOV ANDREYEVNA *and* CHARLOTTA IVANOVNA.)

LYUBOV (*hums the Lezginka*). Why is Leonid so long? What can he be doing in town? (*To* DUNYASHA) Offer the musicians some tea.

TROFIMOV. The sale hasn't taken place, most likely.

LYUBOV. It's the wrong time to have the orchestra, and the wrong time to give a dance. Well, never mind (*sits down and hums softly*).

CHARLOTTA (*gives* PISHTCHIK *a pack of cards*). Here's a pack of cards. Think of any card you like.

PISHTCHIK. I've thought of one.

CHARLOTTA. Shuffle the pack now. That's right. Give it here, my dear Mr. Pishtchik. *Ein, zwei, drei*—now look, it's in your breast pocket.

PISHTCHIK (*taking a card out of his breast pocket*). The eight of spades! Perfectly right! (*Wonderingly*) Fancy that now!

CHARLOTTA (*holding pack of cards in her hands, to* TROFIMOV). Tell me quickly which is the top card.

TROFIMOV. Well, the queen of spades.

CHARLOTTA. It is! (*To* PISHTCHIK) Well, which card is uppermost?

PISHTCHIK. The ace of hearts.

CHARLOTTA. It is! (*Claps her hands, pack of cards disappears.*) Ah! what lovely weather it is to-day!

(*A mysterious feminine voice which seems coming out of the floor answers her.* "Oh, yes, it's magnificent weather, madam.")

CHARLOTTA. You are my perfect ideal.

VOICE. And I greatly admire you too, madam.

STATION MASTER (*applauding*). The lady ventriloquist—bravo!

PISHTCHIK (*wonderingly*). Fancy that now! Most enchanting Charlotta Ivanovna. I'm simply in love with you.

CHARLOTTA. In love? (*Shrugging shoulders*) What do you know of love, *guter Mensch, aber schlechter Musikant.*

TROFIMOV (*pats* PISHTCHIK *on the shoulder*). You dear old horse....

CHARLOTTA. Attention, please! Another trick! (*Takes a travelling rug from a chair.*) Here's a very good rug; I want to sell it (*shaking it out*). Doesn't anyone want to buy it?

PISHTCHIK (*wonderingly*). Fancy that!

CHARLOTTA. *Ein, zwei, drei!* (*Quickly picks up rug she has dropped; behind the rug stands* ANYA; *she makes a curtsey, runs to her mother, embraces her and runs back into the larger drawing-room amidst general enthusiasm.*)

LYUBOV (*applauds*). Bravo! Bravo!

CHARLOTTA. Now again! *Ein, zwei, drei!* (*Lifts up the rug; behind the rug stands* VARYA, *bowing.*)

PISHTCHIK (*wonderingly*). Fancy that now!

CHARLOTTA. That's the end (*throws the rug at* PISHTCHIK, *makes a curtsey, runs into the larger drawing-room*).

PISHTCHIK (*hurries after her*). Mischievous creature! Fancy! (*Goes out.*)

LYUBOV. And still Leonid doesn't come. I can't understand what he's doing in the town so long! Why, everything must be over by now. The estate is sold, or the sale has not taken place. Why keep us so long in suspense?

VARYA (*trying to console her*). Uncle's bought it. I feel sure of that.

TROFIMOV (*ironically*). Oh, yes!

VARYA. Great-aunt sent him an authorisation to buy it in her name, and transfer the debt. She's doing it for Anya's sake, and I'm sure God will be merciful. Uncle will buy it.

LYUBOV. My aunt in Yaroslavl sent fifteen thousand to buy the estate in her name, she doesn't trust us—but that's not enough even to pay the arrears (*hides her face in her hands*). My fate is being sealed to-day, my fate ...

TROFIMOV (*teasing* VARYA). Madame Lopahin.

VARYA (*angrily*). Perpetual student! Twice already you've been sent down from the University.

LYUBOV. Why are you angry, Varya? He's teasing you about Lopahin. Well, what of that? Marry Lopahin if you like, he's a good man, and interesting; if you don't want to, don't! Nobody compels you, darling.

VARYA. I must tell you plainly, Mamma, I look at the matter seriously; he's a good man, I like him.

LYUBOV. Well, marry him. I can't see what you're waiting for.

VARYA. Mamma. I can't make him an offer myself. For the last two years, everyone's been talking to me about him. Everyone talks; but he says nothing or else makes a joke. I see what it means. He's growing rich, he's absorbed in business, he has no thoughts for me. If I had money, were it ever so little, if I had only a hundred roubles, I'd throw everything up and go far away. I would go into a nunnery.

TROFIMOV. What bliss!

VARYA (*to* TROFIMOV). A student ought to have sense! (*In a soft tone with tears*) How ugly you've grown, Petya! How old you look! (*To* LYUBOV ANDREYEVNA, *no longer crying*) But I can't do without work, Mamma; I must have something to do every minute.

(*Enter* YASHA.)

YASHA (*hardly restraining his laughter*). Epihodov has broken a billiard cue! (*Goes out.*)

VARYA. What is Epihodov doing here? Who gave him leave to play billiards? I can't make these people out (*goes out*).

LYUBOV. Don't tease her, Petya. You see she has grief enough without that.

TROFIMOV. She is so very officious, meddling in what's not her business. All the summer she's given Anya and me no peace. She's afraid of a love affair between us. What's it to do with her? Besides, I have given no grounds for it. Such triviality is not in my line. We are above love!

LYUBOV. And I suppose I am beneath love. (*Very uneasily*) Why is it Leonid's not here? If only I could know whether the estate is sold or not! It seems such an incredible calamity that I really don't know what to think. I am distracted . . . I shall scream in a minute . . . I shall do something stupid. Save me, Petya, tell me something, talk to me!

TROFIMOV. What does it matter whether the estate is sold to-day or not? That's all done with long ago. There's no turning back, the path is overgrown. Don't worry yourself, dear Lyubov Andreyevna. You mustn't deceive yourself; for once in your life you must face the truth!

LYUBOV. What truth? You see where the truth lies, but I seem to have lost my sight, I see nothing. You settle every great problem so boldly, but tell me, my dear boy, isn't it because you're young—because you haven't yet understood one of your problems through suffering? You look forward boldly, and isn't it that you don't see and don't expect anything dreadful because life is still hidden from your young eyes? You're bolder, more honest, deeper than we are, but think, be just a little magnanimous, have pity on me. I was born here, you know, my father and mother lived here, my grandfather lived here, I love this house. I can't conceive of life without the cherry orchard, and if it really must be sold, then sell me with the orchard (*embraces* TROFIMOV, *kisses him on the forehead*). My boy was drowned here (*weeps*). Pity me, my dear kind fellow.

TROFIMOV. You know I feel for you with all my heart.

LYUBOV. But that should have been said differently, so differently (*takes out her handkerchief, telegram falls on the floor*). My heart is so heavy to-day. It's so noisy here, my soul is quivering at every sound, I'm shuddering all over, but I can't go away; I'm afraid to be quiet and alone. Don't be hard on me, Petya . . . I love you as though you were one of ourselves. I would gladly let you marry Anya— I swear I would—only, my dear boy, you must take your degree, you do nothing—you're simply tossed by fate from place to place.

That's so strange. It is, isn't it? And you must do something with your beard to make it grow somehow (*laughs*). You look so funny!

TROFIMOV (*picks up the telegram*). I've no wish to be a beauty.

LYUBOV. That's a telegram from Paris. I get one every day. One yesterday and one to-day. That savage creature is ill again, he's in trouble again. He begs forgiveness, beseeches me to go, and really I ought to go to Paris to see him. You look shocked, Petya. What am I to do, my dear boy, what am I to do? He is ill, he is alone and unhappy, and who'll look after him, who'll keep him from doing the wrong thing, who'll give him his medicine at the right time? And why hide it or be silent? I love him, that's clear. I love him! I love him! He's a millstone about my neck, I'm going to the bottom with him, but I love that stone and can't live without it (*presses* TROFIMOV's *hand*). Don't think ill of me, Petya, don't tell me anything, don't tell me …

TROFIMOV (*through his tears*). For God's sake forgive my frankness: why, he robbed you!

LYUBOV. No! No! No! You mustn't speak like that (*covers her ears*).

TROFIMOV. He is a wretch! You're the only person that doesn't know it! He's a worthless creature! A despicable wretch!

LYUBOV (*getting angry, but speaking with restraint*). You're twenty-six or twenty-seven years old, but you're still a schoolboy.

TROFIMOV. Possibly.

LYUBOV. You should be a man at your age! You should understand what love means! And you ought to be in love yourself. You ought to fall in love! (*Angrily*) Yes, yes, and it's not purity in you, you're simply a prude, a comic fool, a freak.

TROFIMOV (*in horror*). The things she's saying!

LYUBOV. I am above love! You're not above love, but simply as our Firs here says, "You are a good-for-nothing." At your age not to have a mistress!

TROFIMOV (*in horror*). This is awful! The things she is saying! (*Goes rapidly into the larger drawing-room clutching his head.*) This is awful! I can't stand it! I'm going. (*Goes off, but at once returns.*) All is over between us! (*Goes off into the ante-room.*)

LYUBOV (*shouts after him*). Petya! Wait a minute! You funny creature! I was joking! Petya! (*There is a sound of somebody running quickly down-*

stairs and suddenly falling with a crash. ANYA and VARYA scream, but there
is a sound of laughter at once.)
LYUBOV. What has happened?

(ANYA runs in.)

ANYA (laughing). Petya's fallen downstairs! (Runs out.)
LYUBOV. What a queer fellow that Petya is!

(The Station Master stands in the middle of the larger room and reads "The
Magdalene," by Alexey Tolstoy. They listen to him, but before he has recited
many lines strains of a waltz are heard from the ante-room and the reading is
broken off. All dance. TROFIMOV, ANYA, VARYA and LYUBOV ANDREYEVNA
come in from the ante-room.)

LYUBOV. Come, Petya—come, pure heart! I beg your pardon. Let's
have a dance! (Dances with PETYA.)

(ANYA and VARYA dance. FIRS comes in, puts his stick down near the side door.
YASHA also comes into the drawing-room and looks on at the dancing.)

YASHA. What is it, old man?
FIRS. I don't feel well. In old days we used to have generals, barons and
admirals dancing at our balls, and now we send for the post-office
clerk and the station master and even they're not overanxious to
come. I am getting feeble. The old master, the grandfather, used to
give sealing-wax for all complaints. I have been taking sealing-wax
for twenty years or more. Perhaps that's what's kept me alive.
YASHA. You bore me, old man! (Yawns) It's time you were done with.
FIRS. Ach, you're a good-for-nothing! (Mutters.)

(TROFIMOV and LYUBOV ANDREYEVNA dance in larger room and then on to
the stage.)

LYUBOV. Merci. I'll sit down a little (sits down). I'm tired.

(Enter ANYA.)

ANYA (*excitedly*). There's a man in the kitchen has been saying that the cherry orchard's been sold to-day.

LYUBOV. Sold to whom?

ANYA. He didn't say to whom. He's gone away.

(*She dances with* TROFIMOV, *and they go off into the larger room.*)

YASHA. There was an old man gossiping there, a stranger.

FIRS. Leonid Andreyevitch isn't here yet, he hasn't come back. He has his light overcoat on, *demi-saison,* he'll catch cold for sure. Ach! Foolish young things!

LYUBOV. I feel as though I should die. Go, Yasha, find out to whom it has been sold.

YASHA. But he went away long ago, the old chap (*laughs*).

LYUBOV (*with slight vexation*). What are you laughing at? What are you pleased at?

YASHA. Epihodov is so funny. He's a silly fellow, two and twenty misfortunes.

LYUBOV. Firs, if the estate is sold, where will you go?

FIRS. Where you bid me, there I'll go.

LYUBOV. Why do you look like that? Are you ill? You ought to be in bed.

FIRS. Yes (*ironically*). Me go to bed and who's to wait here? Who's to see to things without me? I'm the only one in all the house.

YASHA (*to* LYUBOV ANDREYEVNA). Lyubov Andreyevna, permit me to make a request of you; if you go back to Paris again, be so kind as to take me with you. It's positively impossible for me to stay here (*looking about him; in an undertone*). There's no need to say it, you see for yourself—an uncivilised country, the people have no morals, and then the dullness! The food in the kitchen's abominable, and then Firs runs after one muttering all sorts of unsuitable words. Take me with you, please do!

(*Enter* PISHTCHIK.)

PISHTCHIK. Allow me to ask you for a waltz, my dear lady. (LYUBOV ANDREYEVNA *goes with him.*) Enchanting lady, I really must borrow of you just 180 roubles (*dances*), only 180 roubles. (*They pass into the larger room.*)

YASHA (*hums softly*). "Knowest thou my soul's emotion."

(*In the larger drawing-room, a figure in a gray top hat and in check trousers is gesticulating and jumping about.* Shouts of "Bravo, Charlotta Ivanovna.")

DUNYASHA (*she has stopped to powder herself*). My young lady tells me to dance. There are plenty of gentlemen, and too few ladies, but dancing makes me giddy and makes my heart beat. Firs, the post-office clerk said something to me just now that quite took my breath away.

(*Music becomes more subdued.*)

FIRS. What did he say to you?

DUNYASHA. He said I was like a flower.

YASHA (*yawns*). What ignorance! (*Goes out.*)

DUNYASHA. Like a flower. I am a girl of such delicate feelings, I am awfully fond of soft speeches.

FIRS. Your head's being turned.

(*Enter* EPIHODOV.)

EPIHODOV. You have no desire to see me, Dunyasha. I might be an insect (*sighs*). Ah! life!

DUNYASHA. What is it you want?

EPIHODOV. Undoubtedly you may be right (*sighs*). But of course, if one looks at it from that point of view, if I may so express myself, you have, excuse my plain speaking, reduced me to a complete state of mind. I know my destiny. Every day some misfortune befalls me and I have long ago grown accustomed to it, so that I look upon my fate with a smile. You gave me your word, and though I——

DUNYASHA. Let us have a talk later, I entreat you, but now leave me in peace, for I am lost in reverie (*plays with her fan*).

EPIHODOV. I have a misfortune every day, and if I may venture to express myself, I merely smile at it, I even laugh.

(VARYA *enters from the larger drawing-room.*)

VARYA. You still have not gone, Epihodov. What a disrespectful creature you are, really! (*To* DUNYASHA) Go along, Dunyasha! (*To* EPIHODOV) First you play billiards and break the cue, then you go wandering about the drawing-room like a visitor!

EPIHODOV. You really cannot, if I may so express myself, call me to account like this.

VARYA. I'm not calling you to account, I'm speaking to you. You do nothing but wander from place to place and don't do your work. We keep you as a counting-house clerk, but what use you are I can't say.

EPIHODOV (*offended*). Whether I work or whether I walk, whether I eat or whether I play billiards, is a matter to be judged by persons of understanding and my elders.

VARYA. You dare to tell me that! (*Firing up*) You dare! You mean to say I've no understanding. Begone from here! This minute!

EPIHODOV (*intimidated*). I beg you to express yourself with delicacy.

VARYA (*beside herself with anger*). This moment! get out! away! (*He goes towards the door, she following him.*) Two and twenty misfortunes! Take yourself off! Don't let me set eyes on you! (EPIHODOV *has gone out, behind the door his voice,* "I shall lodge a complaint against you.") What! You're coming back? (*Snatches up the stick* FIRS *has put down near the door.*) Come! Come! Come! I'll show you! What! you're coming? Then take that! (*She swings the stick, at the very moment that* LOPAHIN *comes in.*)

LOPAHIN. Very much obliged to you!

VARYA (*angrily and ironically*). I beg your pardon!

LOPAHIN. Not at all! I humbly thank you for your kind reception!

VARYA. No need of thanks for it. (*Moves away, then looks round and asks softly*) I haven't hurt you?

LOPAHIN. Oh, no! Not at all! There's an immense bump coming up, though!

VOICES FROM LARGER ROOM. Lopahin has come! Yermolay Alexeyevitch!

PISHTCHIK. What do I see and hear? (*Kisses* LOPAHIN.) There's a whiff of cognac about you, my dear soul, and we're making merry here too!

(*Enter* LYUBOV ANDREYEVNA.)

LYUBOV. Is it you, Yermolay Alexeyevitch? Why have you been so long? Where's Leonid?

LOPAHIN. Leonid Andreyevitch arrived with me. He is coming.

LYUBOV (*in agitation*). Well! Well! Was there a sale? Speak!

LOPAHIN (*embarrassed, afraid of betraying his joy*). The sale was over at four o'clock. We missed our train—had to wait till half-past nine. (*Sighing heavily*) Ugh! I feel a little giddy.

(*Enter* GAEV. *In his right hand he has purchases, with his left hand he is wiping away his tears.*)

LYUBOV. Well, Leonid? What news? (*Impatiently, with tears*) Make haste, for God's sake!

GAEV (*makes her no answer, simply waves his hand. To* FIRS, *weeping*) Here, take them; there's anchovies, Kertch herrings. I have eaten nothing all day. What I have been through! (*Door into the billiard room is open. There is heard a knocking of balls and the voice of* YASHA *saying* "Eighty-seven." GAEV's *expression changes, he leaves off weeping.*) I am fearfully tired. Firs, come and help me change my things (*goes to his own room across the larger drawing-room*).

PISHTCHIK. How about the sale? Tell us, do!

LYUBOV. Is the cherry orchard sold?

LOPAHIN. It is sold.

LYUBOV. Who has bought it?

LOPAHIN. I have bought it. (*A pause.* LYUBOV *is crushed; she would fall down if she were not standing near a chair and table.*)

(VARYA *takes keys from her waist-band, flings them on the floor in middle of drawing-room and goes out.*)

LOPAHIN. I have bought it! Wait a bit, ladies and gentlemen, pray. My head's a bit muddled, I can't speak (*laughs*). We came to the auction.

Deriganov was there already. Leonid Andreyevitch only had 15,000 and Deriganov bid 30,000, besides the arrears, straight off. I saw how the land lay. I bid against him. I bid 40,000, he bid 45,000, I said 55, and so he went on, adding 5 thousands and I adding 10. Well … So it ended. I bid 90, and it was knocked down to me. Now the cherry orchard's mine! Mine! (*Chuckles*) My God, the cherry orchard's mine! Tell me that I'm drunk, that I'm out of my mind, that it's all a dream (*stamps with his feet*). Don't laugh at me! If my father and my grandfather could rise from their graves and see all that has happened! How their Yermolay, ignorant, beaten Yermolay, who used to run about barefoot in winter, how that very Yermolay has bought the finest estate in the world! I have bought the estate where my father and grandfather were slaves, where they weren't even admitted into the kitchen. I am asleep, I am dreaming! It is all fancy, it is the work of your imagination plunged in the darkness of ignorance (*picks up keys, smiling fondly*). She threw away the keys; she means to show she's not the housewife now (*jingles the keys*). Well, no matter. (*The orchestra is heard tuning up.*) Hey, musicians! Play! I want to hear you. Come, all of you, and look how Yermolay Lopahin will take the axe to the cherry orchard, how the trees will fall to the ground! We will build houses on it and our grandsons and great-grandsons will see a new life springing up there. Music! Play up!

(*Music begins to play.* LYUBOV ANDREYEVNA *has sunk into a chair and is weeping bitterly.*)

LOPAHIN (*reproachfully*). Why, why didn't you listen to me? My poor friend! Dear lady, there's no turning back now. (*With tears*) Oh, if all this could be over, oh, if our miserable disjointed life could somehow soon be changed!

PISHTCHIK (*takes him by the arm, in an undertone*). She's weeping, let us go and leave her alone. Come (*takes him by the arm and leads him into the larger drawing-room*).

LOPAHIN. What's that? Musicians, play up! All must be as I wish it. (*With irony*) Here comes the new master, the owner of the cherry orchard! (*Accidentally tips over a little table, almost upsetting the candelabra.*) I can pay for everything! (*Goes out with* PISHTCHIK. *No one re-*

mains on the stage or in the larger drawing-room except LYUBOV, *who sits huddled up, weeping bitterly. The music plays softly.* ANYA *and* TROFIMOV *come in quickly.* ANYA *goes up to her mother and falls on her knees before her.* TROFIMOV *stands at the entrance to the larger drawing-room.*)

ANYA. Mamma! Mamma, you're crying, dear, kind, good Mamma! My precious! I love you! I bless you! The cherry orchard is sold, it is gone, that's true, that's true! But don't weep, Mamma! Life is still before you, you have still your good, pure heart! Let us go, let us go, darling, away from here! We will make a new garden, more splendid than this one; you will see it, you will understand. And joy, quiet, deep joy, will sink into your soul like the sun at evening! And you will smile, Mamma! Come, darling, let us go!

CURTAIN.

ACT IV

SCENE: *Same as in First Act. There are neither curtains on the windows nor pictures on the walls: only a little furniture remains piled up in a corner as if for sale. There is a sense of desolation; near the outer door and in the background of the scene are packed trunks, travelling bags, etc. On the left the door is open, and from here the voices of* VARYA *and* ANYA *are audible.* LOPAHIN *is standing waiting.* YASHA *is holding a tray with glasses full of champagne. In front of the stage* EPIHODOV *is tying up a box. In the background behind the scene a hum of talk from the peasants who have come to say good-bye. The voice of* GAEV: "Thanks, brothers, thanks!"*

YASHA. The peasants have come to say good-bye. In my opinion, Yermolay Alexeyevitch, the peasants are good-natured, but they don't know much about things.

(*The hum of talk dies away. Enter across front of stage* LYUBOV ANDREYEVNA *and* GAEV. *She is not weeping, but is pale; her face is quivering—she cannot speak.*)

GAEV. You gave them your purse, Lyuba. That won't do—that won't do!
LYUBOV. I couldn't help it! I couldn't help it!

(*Both go out.*)

LOPAHIN (*in the doorway, calls after them*). You will take a glass at parting? Please do. I didn't think to bring any from the town, and at the station I could only get one bottle. Please take a glass (*a pause*). What? You don't care for any? (*Comes away from the door.*) If I'd known, I wouldn't have bought it. Well, and I'm not going to drink it.

(YASHA *carefully sets the tray down on a chair.*) You have a glass, Yasha, anyway.

YASHA. Good luck to the travellers, and luck to those that stay behind! (*Drinks.*) This champagne isn't the real thing, I can assure you.

LOPAHIN. It cost eight roubles the bottle (*a pause*). It's devilish cold here.

YASHA. They haven't heated the stove to-day—it's all the same since we're going (*laughs*).

LOPAHIN. What are you laughing for?

YASHA. For pleasure.

LOPAHIN. Though it's October, it's as still and sunny as though it were summer. It's just right for building! (*Looks at his watch; says in doorway*) Take note, ladies and gentlemen, the train goes in forty-seven minutes; so you ought to start for the station in twenty minutes. You must hurry up!

(TROFIMOV *comes in from out of doors wearing a great-coat.*)

TROFIMOV. I think it must be time to start, the horses are ready. The devil only knows what's become of my goloshes; they're lost. (*In the doorway*) Anya! My goloshes aren't here. I can't find them.

LOPAHIN. And I'm getting off to Harkov. I am going in the same train with you. I'm spending all the winter at Harkov. I've been wasting all my time gossiping with you and fretting with no work to do. I can't get on without work. I don't know what to do with my hands, they flap about so queerly, as if they didn't belong to me.

TROFIMOV. Well, we're just going away, and you will take up your profitable labours again.

LOPAHIN. Do take a glass.

TROFIMOV. No, thanks.

LOPAHIN. Then you're going to Moscow now?

TROFIMOV. Yes. I shall see them as far as the town, and to-morrow I shall go on to Moscow.

LOPAHIN. Yes, I daresay, the professors aren't giving any lectures, they're waiting for your arrival.

TROFIMOV. That's not your business.

LOPAHIN. How many years have you been at the University?

TROFIMOV. Do think of something newer than that—that's stale and flat (*hunts for goloshes*). You know we shall most likely never see each other again, so let me give you one piece of advice at parting: don't wave your arms about—get out of the habit. And another thing, building villas, reckoning up that the summer visitors will in time become independent farmers—reckoning like that, that's not the thing to do either. After all, I am fond of you: you have fine delicate fingers like an artist, you've a fine delicate soul.

LOPAHIN (*embraces him*). Good-bye, my dear fellow. Thanks for everything. Let me give you money for the journey, if you need it.

TROFIMOV. What for? I don't need it.

LOPAHIN. Why, you haven't got a halfpenny.

TROFIMOV. Yes, I have, thank you. I got some money for a translation. Here it is in my pocket, (*anxiously*) but where can my goloshes be!

VARYA (*from the next room*). Take the nasty things! (*Flings a pair of goloshes on to the stage.*)

TROFIMOV. Why are you so cross, Varya? h'm!... but those aren't my goloshes.

LOPAHIN. I sowed three thousand acres with poppies in the spring, and now I have cleared forty thousand profit. And when my poppies were in flower, wasn't it a picture! So here, as I say, I made forty thousand, and I'm offering you a loan because I can afford to. Why turn up your nose? I am a peasant—I speak bluntly.

TROFIMOV. Your father was a peasant, mine was a chemist—and that proves absolutely nothing whatsoever. (LOPAHIN *takes out his pocketbook.*) Stop that—stop that. If you were to offer me two hundred thousand I wouldn't take it. I am an independent man, and everything that all of you, rich and poor alike, prize so highly and hold so dear, hasn't the slightest power over me—it's like so much fluff fluttering in the air. I can get on without you. I can pass by you. I am strong and proud. Humanity is advancing towards the highest truth, the highest happiness, which is possible on earth, and I am in the front ranks.

LOPAHIN. Will you get there?

TROFIMOV. I shall get there (*a pause*). I shall get there, or I shall show others the way to get there.

(*In the distance is heard the stroke of an axe on a tree.*)

LOPAHIN. Good-bye, my dear fellow; it's time to be off. We turn up our noses at one another, but life is passing all the while. When I am working hard without resting, then my mind is more at ease, and it seems to me as though I too know what I exist for; but how many people there are in Russia, my dear boy, who exist, one doesn't know what for. Well, it doesn't matter. That's not what keeps things spinning. They tell me Leonid Andreyevitch has taken a situation. He is going to be a clerk at the bank—6,000 roubles a year. Only, of course, he won't stick to it—he's too lazy.

ANYA (*in the doorway*). Mamma begs you not to let them chop down the orchard until she's gone.

TROFIMOV. Yes, really, you might have the tact (*walks out across the front of the stage*).

LOPAHIN. I'll see to it! I'll see to it! Stupid fellows! (*Goes out after him.*)

ANYA. Has Firs been taken to the hospital?

YASHA. I told them this morning. No doubt they have taken him.

ANYA (*to EPIHODOV, who passes across the drawing-room*). Semyon Pantaleyevitch, inquire, please, if Firs has been taken to the hospital.

YASHA (*in a tone of offence*). I told Yegor this morning—why ask a dozen times?

EPIHODOV. Firs is advanced in years. It's my conclusive opinion no treatment would do him good; it's time he was gathered to his fathers. And I can only envy him (*puts a trunk down on a cardboard hatbox and crushes it*). There, now, of course—I knew it would be so.

YASHA (*jeeringly*). Two and twenty misfortunes!

VARYA (*through the door*). Has Firs been taken to the hospital?

ANYA. Yes.

VARYA. Why wasn't the note for the doctor taken too?

ANYA. Oh, then, we must send it after them (*goes out*).

VARYA (*from the adjoining room*). Where's Yasha? Tell him his mother's come to say good-bye to him.

YASHA (*waves his hand*). They put me out of all patience! (DUNYASHA *has all this time been busy about the luggage. Now, when* YASHA *is left alone, she goes up to him.*)

DUNYASHA. You might just give me one look, Yasha. You're going away. You're leaving me (*weeps and throws herself on his neck*).

YASHA. What are you crying for? (*Drinks the champagne.*) In six days I shall be in Paris again. To-morrow we shall get into the express train and roll away in a flash. I can scarcely believe it! *Vive la France!* It doesn't suit me here—it's not the life for me; there's no doing anything. I have seen enough of the ignorance here. I have had enough of it (*drinks champagne*). What are you crying for? Behave yourself properly, and then you won't cry.

DUNYASHA (*powders her face, looking in a pocket-mirror*). Do send me a letter from Paris. You know how I loved you, Yasha—how I loved you! I am a tender creature, Yasha.

YASHA. Here they are coming!

(*Busies himself about the trunks, humming softly. Enter* LYUBOV AN-DREYEVNA, GAEV, ANYA *and* CHARLOTTA IVANOVNA.)

GAEV. We ought to be off. There's not much time now (*looking at* YASHA). What a smell of herrings!

LYUBOV. In ten minutes we must get into the carriage (*casts a look about the room*). Farewell, dear house, dear old home of our fathers! Winter will pass and spring will come, and then you will be no more; they will tear you down! How much those walls have seen! (*Kisses her daughter passionately.*) My treasure, how bright you look! Your eyes are sparkling like diamonds! Are you glad? Very glad?

ANYA. Very glad! A new life is beginning, Mamma.

GAEV. Yes, really, everything is all right now. Before the cherry orchard was sold, we were all worried and wretched, but afterwards, when once the question was settled conclusively, irrevocably, we all felt calm and even cheerful. I am a bank clerk now—I am a financier—cannon off the red. And you, Lyuba, after all, you are looking better; there's no question of that.

LYUBOV. Yes. My nerves are better, that's true. (*Her hat and coat are handed to her.*) I'm sleeping well. Carry out my things, Yasha. It's time. (*To* ANYA) My darling, we shall soon see each other again. I am going to Paris. I can live there on the money your Yaroslavl auntie sent us to buy the estate with—hurrah for auntie!—but that money won't last long.

ANYA. You'll come back soon, Mamma, won't you? I'll be working up for my examination in the high school, and when I have passed that, I shall set to work and be a help to you. We will read all sorts of things together, Mamma, won't we? (*Kisses her mother's hands.*) We will read in the autumn evenings. We'll read lots of books, and a new wonderful world will open out before us (*dreamily*). Mamma, come soon.

LYUBOV. I shall come, my precious treasure (*embraces her*).

(*Enter* LOPAHIN. CHARLOTTA *softly hums a song.*)

GAEV. Charlotta's happy; she's singing!

CHARLOTTA (*picks up a bundle like a swaddled baby*). Bye, bye, my baby. (*A baby is heard crying: "Ooah! ooah!"*) Hush, hush, my pretty boy! (*"Ooah! ooah!"*) Poor little thing! (*Throws the bundle back.*) You must please find me a situation. I can't go on like this.

LOPAHIN. We'll find you one, Charlotta Ivanovna. Don't you worry yourself.

GAEV. Everyone's leaving us. Varya's going away. We have become of no use all at once.

CHARLOTTA. There's nowhere for me to be in the town. I must go away. (*Hums*) What care I ...

(*Enter* PISHTCHIK.)

LOPAHIN. The freak of nature!

PISHTCHIK (*gasping*). Oh! ... let me get my breath.... I'm worn out ... my most honoured ... Give me some water.

GAEV. Want some money, I suppose? Your humble servant! I'll go out of the way of temptation (*goes out*).

PISHTCHIK. It's a long while since I have been to see you ... dearest lady. (*To* LOPAHIN) You are here ... glad to see you ... a man of immense intellect ... take ... here (*gives* LOPAHIN) 400 roubles. That leaves me owing 840.

LOPAHIN (*shrugging his shoulders in amazement*). It's like a dream. Where did you get it?

PISHTCHIK. Wait a bit ... I'm hot ... a most extraordinary occurrence! Some Englishmen came along and found in my land some sort of white clay. (*To* LYUBOV ANDREYEVNA) And 400 for you ... most lovely ... wonderful (*gives money*). The rest later (*sips water*). A young man in the train was telling me just now that a great philosopher advises jumping off a house-top. "Jump!" says he; "the whole gist of the problem lies in that." (*Wonderingly*) Fancy that, now! Water, please!

LOPAHIN. What Englishmen?

PISHTCHIK. I have made over to them the rights to dig the clay for twenty-four years ... and now, excuse me ... I can't stay ... I must be trotting on. I'm going to Znoikovo ... to Kardamanovo.... I'm in debt all round (*sips*).... To your very good health! ... I'll come in on Thursday.

LYUBOV. We are just off to the town, and to-morrow I start for abroad.

PISHTCHIK. What! (*In agitation*) Why to the town? Oh, I see the furniture ... the boxes. No matter ... (*through his tears*) ... no matter ... men of enormous intellect ... these Englishmen.... Never mind ... be happy. God will succour you ... no matter ... everything in this world must have an end (*kisses* LYUBOV ANDREYEVNA'S *hand*). If the rumour reaches you that my end has come, think of this ... old horse, and say: "There once was such a man in the world ... Semyonov-Pishtchik ... the Kingdom of Heaven be his!" ... most extraordinary weather ... yes. (*Goes out in violent agitation, but at once returns and says in the doorway*) Dashenka wishes to be remembered to you (*goes out*).

LYUBOV. Now we can start. I leave with two cares in my heart. The first is leaving Firs ill. (*Looking at her watch*) We have still five minutes.

ANYA. Mamma, Firs has been taken to the hospital. Yasha sent him off this morning.

LYUBOV. My other anxiety is Varya. She is used to getting up early and working; and now, without work, she's like a fish out of water. She is thin and pale, and she's crying, poor dear! (*A pause.*) You are well aware, Yermolay Alexeyevitch, I dreamed of marrying her to you, and everything seemed to show that you would get married (*whispers to* ANYA *and motions to* CHARLOTTA *and both go out*). She loves you—she suits you. And I don't know—I don't know why it is you seem, as it were, to avoid each other. I can't understand it!

LOPAHIN. I don't understand it myself, I confess. It's queer somehow, altogether. If there's still time, I'm ready now at once. Let's settle it straight off, and go ahead; but without you, I feel I shan't make her an offer.

LYUBOV. That's excellent. Why, a single moment's all that's necessary. I'll call her at once.

LOPAHIN. And there's champagne all ready too (*looking into the glasses*). Empty! Someone's emptied them already. (YASHA *coughs.*) I call that greedy.

LYUBOV (*eagerly*). Capital! We will go out. Yasha, *allez!* I'll call her in. (*At the door*) Varya, leave all that; come here. Come along! (*goes out with* YASHA).

LOPAHIN (*looking at his watch*). Yes.

(*A pause. Behind the door, smothered laughter and whispering, and, at last, enter* VARYA.)

VARYA (*looking a long while over the things*). It is strange, I can't find it anywhere.

LOPAHIN. What are you looking for?

VARYA. I packed it myself, and I can't remember (*a pause*).

LOPAHIN. Where are you going now, Varvara Mihailova?

VARYA. I? To the Ragulins. I have arranged to go to them to look after the house—as a housekeeper.

LOPAHIN. That's in Yashnovo? It'll be seventy miles away (*a pause*). So this is the end of life in this house!

VARYA (*looking among the things*). Where is it? Perhaps I put it in the trunk. Yes, life in this house is over—there will be no more of it.

LOPAHIN. And I'm just off to Harkov—by this next train. I've a lot of business there. I'm leaving Epihodov here, and I've taken him on.

VARYA. Really!

LOPAHIN. This time last year we had snow already, if you remember;

but now it's so fine and sunny. Though it's cold, to be sure—three degrees of frost.

VARYA. I haven't looked (*a pause*). And besides, our thermometer's broken (*a pause*).

(*Voice at the door from the yard:* "Yermolay Alexeyevitch!")

LOPAHIN (*as though he had long been expecting this summons*). This minute!

(LOPAHIN *goes out quickly.* VARYA *sitting on the floor and laying her head on a bag full of clothes, sobs quietly. The door opens.* LYUBOV ANDREYEVNA *comes in cautiously.*)

LYUBOV. Well? (*A pause.*) We must be going.

VARYA (*has wiped her eyes and is no longer crying*). Yes, Mamma, it's time to start. I shall have time to get to the Ragulins to-day, if only you're not late for the train.

LYUBOV (*in the doorway*). Anya, put your things on.

(*Enter* ANYA, *then* GAEV *and* CHARLOTTA IVANOVNA. GAEV *has on a warm coat with a hood. Servants and cabmen come in.* EPIHODOV *bustles about the luggage.*)

LYUBOV. Now we can start on our travels.

ANYA (*joyfully*). On our travels!

GAEV. My friends—my dear, my precious friends! Leaving this house for ever, can I be silent? Can I refrain from giving utterance at leave-taking to those emotions which now flood all my being?

ANYA (*supplicatingly*). Uncle!

VARYA. Uncle, you mustn't!

GAEV (*dejectedly*). Cannon and into the pocket . . . I'll be quiet. . . .

(*Enter* TROFIMOV *and afterwards* LOPAHIN.)

TROFIMOV. Well, ladies and gentlemen, we must start.

LOPAHIN. Epihodov, my coat!

LYUBOV. I'll stay just one minute. It seems as though I have never seen before what the walls, what the ceilings in this house were like, and now I look at them with greediness, with such tender love.

GAEV. I remember when I was six years old sitting in that window on Trinity Day watching my father going to church.

LYUBOV. Have all the things been taken?

LOPAHIN. I think all. (*Putting on overcoat, to* EPIHODOV) You, Epihodov, mind you see everything is right.

EPIHODOV (*in a husky voice*). Don't you trouble, Yermolay Alexeyevitch.

LOPAHIN. Why, what's wrong with your voice?

EPIHODOV. I've just had a drink of water, and I choked over something.

YASHA (*contemptuously*). The ignorance!

LYUBOV. We are going—and not a soul will be left here.

LOPAHIN. Not till the spring.

VARYA (*pulls a parasol out of a bundle, as though about to hit someone with it.* LOPAHIN *makes a gesture as though alarmed*). What is it? I didn't mean anything.

TROFIMOV. Ladies and gentlemen, let us get into the carriage. It's time. The train will be in directly.

VARYA. Petya, here they are, your goloshes, by that box. (*With tears*) And what dirty old things they are!

TROFIMOV (*putting on his goloshes*). Let us go, friends!

GAEV (*greatly agitated, afraid of weeping*). The train—the station! Double baulk, ah!

LYUBOV. Let us go!

LOPAHIN. Are we all here? (*Locks the side-door on left.*) The things are all here. We must lock up. Let us go!

ANYA. Good-bye, home! Good-bye to the old life!

TROFIMOV. Welcome to the new life!

(TROFIMOV *goes out with* ANYA. VARYA *looks round the room and goes out slowly.* YASHA *and* CHARLOTTA IVANOVNA, *with her dog, go out.*)

LOPAHIN. Till the spring, then! Come, friends, till we meet! (*Goes out.*)

(LYUBOV ANDREYEVNA *and* GAEV *remain alone. As though they had been waiting for this, they throw themselves on each other's necks, and break into subdued smothered sobbing, afraid of being overheard.*)

GAEV (*in despair*). Sister, my sister!

LYUBOV. Oh, my orchard!—my sweet, beautiful orchard! My life, my youth, my happiness, good-bye! good-bye!

VOICE OF ANYA (*calling gaily*). Mamma!

VOICE OF TROFIMOV (*gaily, excitedly*). Aa—oo!

LYUBOV. One last look at the walls, at the windows. My dear mother loved to walk about this room.

GAEV. Sister, sister!

VOICE OF ANYA. Mamma!

VOICE OF TROFIMOV. Aa—oo!

LYUBOV. We are coming. (*They go out.*)

(*The stage is empty. There is the sound of the doors being locked up, then of the carriages driving away. There is silence. In the stillness there is the dull stroke of an axe in a tree, clanging with a mournful lonely sound. Footsteps are heard. FIRS appears in the doorway on the right. He is dressed as always—in a pea-jacket and white waistcoat, with slippers on his feet. He is ill.*)

FIRS (*goes up to the doors, and tries the handles*). Locked! They have gone . . . (*sits down on sofa*). They have forgotten me. . . . Never mind . . . I'll sit here a bit. . . . I'll be bound Leonid Andreyevitch hasn't put his fur coat on and has gone off in his thin overcoat (*sighs anxiously*). I didn't see after him. . . . These young people . . . (*mutters something that can't be distinguished*). Life has slipped by as though I hadn't lived. (*Lies down*) I'll lie down a bit. . . . There's no strength in you, nothing left you—all gone! Ech! I'm good for nothing (*lies motionless*).

(*A sound is heard that seems to come from the sky, like a breaking harp-string, dying away mournfully. All is still again, and there is heard nothing but the strokes of the axe far away in the orchard.*)

CURTAIN.

A NOTE ON THE TYPE

The principal text of this Modern Library edition was set in a digitized version of Janson, a typeface that dates from about 1690 and was cut by Nicholas Kis, a Hungarian working in Amsterdam. The original matrices have survived and are held by the Stempel foundry in Germany. Hermann Zapf redesigned some of the weights and sizes for Stempel, basing his revisions on the original design.